Praise for *The Best American Poetry*

"Each year, a vivid snapshot of what a distinguished poet finds exciting, fresh, and memorable: and over the years, as good a comprehensive overview of contemporary poetry as there can be."

—Robert Pinsky

"*The Best American Poetry* series has become one of the mainstays of the poetry publication world. For each volume, a guest editor is enlisted to cull the collective output of large and small literary journals published that year to select seventy-five of the year's 'best' poems. The guest editor is also asked to write an introduction to the collection, and the anthologies would be indispensable for these essays alone; combined with [David] Lehman's 'state-of-poetry' forewords and the guest editors' introductions, these anthologies seem to capture the zeitgeist of the current attitudes in American poetry."

—Academy of American Poets

"A high volume of poetic greatness . . . in all of these volumes . . . there is brilliance, there is innovation, there are surprises."

—*Publishers Weekly* (starred review)

"A year's worth of the very best!"

—*People*

"A preponderance of intelligent, straightforward poems."

—*Booklist*

"Certainly it attests to poetry's continuing vitality."

—*Publishers Weekly* (starred review)

"A 'best' anthology that really lives up to its title."

—*Chicago Tribune*

"An essential purchase."

—*The Washington Post*

"For the small community of American poets, *The Best American Poetry* is the *Michelin Guide*, the *Reader's Digest*, and the Prix Goncourt."

—*L'Observateur*

THE
BEST
AMERICAN
POETRY
2023

◇ ◇ ◇

Elaine Equi, Editor

David Lehman, Series Editor

SCRIBNER POETRY

NEW YORK   LONDON   TORONTO   SYDNEY   NEW DELHI

Scribner Poetry
An Imprint of Simon & Schuster, Inc.
1230 Avenue of the Americas
New York, NY 10020

First Scribner Poetry edition September 2023

SCRIBNER POETRY and design are registered trademarks of The Gale Group, Inc.,
used under license by Simon & Schuster, Inc., the publisher of this work.

For information about special discounts for bulk purchases, please contact Simon &
Schuster Special Sales at 1-866-506-1949 or business@simonandschuster.com.

The Simon & Schuster Speakers Bureau can bring authors to your live event.
For more information or to book an event, contact the Simon & Schuster Speakers
Bureau at 1-866-248-3049 or visit our website at www.simonspeakers.com.

Manufactured in the United States of America

1   3   5   7   9   10   8   6   4   2

Library of Congress Control Number: 88644281

ISBN 978-1-9821-8676-0
ISBN 978-1-9821-8675-3 (pbk)
ISBN 978-1-9821-8677-7 (ebook)

CONTENTS

DAVID LEHMAN was born in New York City. Educated at Stuyvesant High School and Columbia University, he spent two years at Clare College, Cambridge, as a Kellett Fellow, and worked as Lionel Trilling's research assistant upon his return from England. He received his PhD at Columbia and taught for four years at Hamilton College. After a postdoctoral fellowship at Cornell, he turned to writing as a full-time occupation. Lehman launched *The Best American Poetry* series in 1988. *The Morning Line* (University of Pittsburgh Press, 2021) is the most recent of his poetry collections; his prose books include *The Mysterious Romance of Murder: Crime, Detection, and the Spirit of Noir* (Cornell University Press, 2022), *One Hundred Autobiographies: A Memoir,* and *Signs of the Times: Deconstruction and the Fall of Paul de Man.* In 2010 he received the Deems Taylor Award from the American Society of Composers, Authors, and Publishers (ASCAP) for *A Fine Romance: Jewish Songwriters, American Songs.* Lehman lives in New York City and in Ithaca, New York.

FOREWORD

by David Lehman

◊   ◊   ◊

Oscar Wilde loaned me the pair of aesthetes who conducted the dialogue in his wonderful essay "The Critic as Artist." Here's their playful take on contemporary poetry:

GILBERT: You poets are incorrigible optimists.

ERNEST: What makes you say so? Aren't poets always complaining that no one reads their work?

GILBERT: With some justice, too. Poetry is in a state of perennial deflation: unlimited supply, low demand, and high unemployment.

ERNEST: Brad Leithauser says as much in his book *Rhyme's Rooms: The Architecture of Poetry*. He says the "possible 'decline' of the role of poetry in American life" is the longest lasting subject of academic discussion.

GILBERT: That's optimism for you.

ERNEST: How so?

GILBERT: The economics are lousy, yet you guys are always writing books *about* poetry, as if it were a going concern. One book suggests that everyone can write the stuff; a second argues that the hatred of poetry is a poet's prerequisite, a third feels that it's okay to hate poetry but spare some love for poems. A recent article contends that T. S. Eliot killed poetry with *The Waste Land*. What's Mr. Leithauser's take?

ERNEST: The title itself is an echo of John Hollander's *Rhyme's Reason*, arguably the best book out there for the novice.

GILBERT: Hollander exemplified the forms in addition to defining them. Is that what Leithauser does?

ERNEST: No, but he introduced me to a great poem by Malcolm Lowry called "Strange Type":

I wrote: in the dark cavern of our birth.
The printer had it tavern, which seems better:
But herein lies the subject of our mirth,
Since on the next page death appears as dearth.
So it may be that God's word was distraction,
Which to our strange type appears destruction,
Which is bitter.

GILBERT: That's an admirable piece of writing. What does the author say about it?

ERNEST: He dwells on the postponed rhyme of "better" and "bitter."

GILBERT: Nice to think that some poets still know about rhyme, meter, and form, and can make the case for constrictive forms.

ERNEST: Yes, he's the rare reader who appreciates the rhyme of "sultry" and "adultery."

GILBERT: Byron is underrated, isn't he? Don't you love the rhymes in *Don Juan*? "But—Oh! ye lords of ladies intellectual, / Inform us truly, have they not hen-pecked you all?"

ERNEST: Yes and yes. But the best chapter in the book is about song lyrics, which Leithauser writes about with passion, acumen, and good taste: lyrics by Lorenz Hart, Cole Porter, Irving Berlin.

GILBERT: Thank you for recommending *Rhyme's Rooms*. May I borrow it for the weekend?

ERNEST: Yes, but it won't necessarily support your thesis that poets are optimistic.

GILBERT: You poets are a disputatious lot.

★★★

The major event of 2022, Russia's invasion of Ukraine on February 24, is but one distressing fact among the many competing for attention in a year marked by Covid variants, pandemic fatigue, runaway inflation, horrific hurricanes and wildfires, a plethora of controversies and scandals, bad behavior, civic unrest, and the most polarized populace in my lifetime.

Poetry still makes news, even if sometimes the news brings no relief. In May 2022 a friend alerted me to this ungainly tabloid headline: "University of Salford cancels SONNETS from writing course because they are 'products of white Western culture' amid push to 'decolonise the curriculum'." At first I thought this was a joke on a par with "Drop Box Outside National Archives Allows Ex-Presidents to Anonymously Return Classified Documents" in a satirical publication like *The Onion*. But I looked it up, and Britain's *Telegraph* of May 14, 2022, got there three days ahead of the *Daily Mail* with the report that the University of Salford had "sidelined" the sonnet. A great sonnet is its own best defense. Take Shakespeare's, number 29:

> When, in disgrace with fortune and men's eyes,
> I all alone beweep my outcast state,
> And trouble deaf heaven with my bootless cries,
> And look upon myself and curse my fate,
> Wishing me like to one more rich in hope,
> Featured like him, like him with friends possessed,
> Desiring this man's art and that man's scope,
> With what I most enjoy contented least;
> Yet in these thoughts myself almost despising,
> Haply I think on thee, and then my state,
> (Like to the lark at break of day arising
> From sullen earth) sings hymns at heaven's gate;
> > For thy sweet love remembered such wealth brings
> > That then I scorn to change my state with kings.

The unhappy speaker, friendless and alone, envious of others, sorry for himself, wallows in his "outcast state" until chance ("hap") favors him with thoughts of "thee" and "thy sweet love," which act upon him "Like to the lark at break of day arising / From sullen earth," a gorgeous simile. In the time-honored fashion of the sonnet, the "Yet" that begins line nine signals the pivot to a blessed "state" powerful enough to neutralize the list of woes in the first eight lines. Bad fortune turns to good—thanks to the agency of the form and the craft and eloquence of the sonneteer.

With weapons provided by critical theory, it would not be impossible to seize upon the words "wealth" and "kings" in the closing couplet and claim that the poem sneakily addresses the subject of monetary metals in the mercantile era. But it would be perverse.

A reminder of poetry's enduring value comes from an article in *The New York Times* from war correspondent Alissa J. Rubin, a fifteen-year *Times* veteran who has served as the paper's bureau chief in Baghdad, Kabul, and Paris. Asked what she reads when she reports from a war zone, she mentions *The Iliad*, singling out Achilles' visit to Priam's hut as particularly stirring. She also names a pair of Auden poems ("Musée des Beaux Arts," "September 1, 1939"), and William Butler Yeats's "Nineteen Hundred and Nineteen." Not an anthology standard, the Yeats poem is ambitious and challenging, and I found it heartening that Ms. Rubin, operating in the heart of danger under deadline pressure, never travels without a selected Yeats and a selected Auden.

★★★

The series editor of *The Best American Poetry* performs many functions, none more important than selecting the year's guest editor.

Elaine Equi always makes me want to write poems, not because she makes it look enjoyable (which she does) but because she sees the poetic possibility in a situation ("It was fun to meet you and live briefly in your novel"), a conjunction of sounds ("Indigo lasso"), or an alternative universe ("If I Weren't a Poet, I'd Be a Bouncer"). The openings of her poems hook you: "You look familiar. / Were you once my mother?" "Step right up and speak into the void," and "Some prayers are spontaneous exclamations" (all from *The Intangibles*, her 2019 book). The virtues of her work include the use of minimal means to achieve maximum effects, the poetic value of the American vernacular, humor, and surprise. "A poet is someone who goes out of her way to preserve / a mystery," she notes in a poem about murder mysteries. But she also writes, she tells us in "Why," "to spite an old nun who punished me for telling the truth by having me write 'I will not tell lies' one hundred times."

As an editor, Elaine distinguished herself with her enthusiasm, assiduousness, and decisiveness. We began the process of reading and evaluating earlier than usual to compensate for the supply-chain disruptions that have become endemic since Covid and that have wreaked havoc on production schedules. We have the delicious surprise of a previously unpublished poem by W. H. Auden. We have exciting first-timers; a quartet of former *BAP* editors (Gerstler, Hayes, Komunyakaa, Zapruder); the current U.S. Poet Laureate (Ada Limón), the winner of the 2022 Pulitzer Prize (Diane Seuss), as well as esteemed poets never before represented in the *BAP* series (Boris Dralyuk, Vincent Katz, Michael Lally, and Maureen N. McLane among them). You'll find prose poems, a villanelle, a biographical poem, and a cento. As a whole, the collection testifies to the strength of the New York School in American poetry. Equi adds a twist with her loyalty to the adage Polonius issues in *Hamlet*: "Brevity is the soul of wit."

★★★

Richard Howard died on the last day of March 2022. How rich a literary life he led. Many have reason to mourn his loss. Richard faithfully mentored young students of poetry as if fulfilling a civic duty. Readers of French literature owe him a special debt, for he translated so much of it: more than 150 books in all, including works by Baudelaire, Barthes, de Beauvoir, Gide, Michaux, Stendhal, and Paul Valéry, as well as the memoirs of Charles de Gaulle.

Back in 1978, Richard invited me to visit him in his fifth-floor apartment in a building called the Waverly Mews near Washington Square Park in New York City. It was wall-to-wall books, except for the bathroom where photographs of writers and artists covered every inch of wall and ceiling. Richard told me he had learned French in five days from a Viennese aunt on an automobile trip from Cleveland to Miami. He often said things that one wanted to record.

Eliot said Henry James had a mind too fine for an idea to violate it, not a problem Eliot suffered from . . .

I was a cocky young assistant professor at Hamilton College in Clinton, New York, where I had a brutal teaching schedule but got to run the readings and lectures series. That October Richard came to Hamilton to give a poetry reading and two lectures—"The Art of

Digression" and "The Art of Boredom." In my pocket notebook I wrote down the aphorisms that came tripping off his tongue: "*Innocence versus experience is Blake's way of presenting Oedipus and the Sphinx.*" "*The root of influence is astrological and is related to influenza.*" At the airport waiting for the plane that would return him to New York City, Richard entertained me and my colleague Joel Black by reading aloud one of his *Two-Part Inventions*, "Wildflowers," in which Oscar Wilde meets Walt Whitman and they duel in verse.

Henry James does to language what art does to life . . .

Richard was one of poetry's great pinch-hitters. In Y2K Star Black and I scheduled John Hollander for a Monday night poetry reading at KGB Bar, but John wasn't feeling well enough to come to the city from New Haven, so Richard volunteered to read the work of his friend from undergraduate days at Columbia University. In 2003, he agreed to teach a literature seminar at the New School when the regular faculty member had to cancel on the eve of opening day.

In this course we will consider the discrepancy between the name and the adjective derived from it: Socratic, Platonic, Christian, Machiavellian, Elizabethan, Byronic, Marxist, Victorian, Freudian, Kafkaesque . . .

Richard's syllabi for the seminars he gave at Columbia and elsewhere are inventive, reflecting his erudition and wide-ranging curiosity, and I would like someday to gather and publish them in a literary journal of note.

Prose is to bread as verse is to cake . . .

At one time or another Richard served as poetry editor of *New American Writing, Shenandoah, Western Humanities Review, The New Republic,* and *The Paris Review.* Mark Strand cracked that Richard needs to be poetry editor of at least two magazines concurrently. When I launched *The Best American Poetry* in 1988, I knew I could count on Richard to discover fresh talent and help it make its way. Inevitably, I asked him to make the selections for the 1995 volume.

The difference between prose and verse is simple: "Prose proceeds, verse reverses."

In the early 1990s, Richard spent each fall on the faculty at the University of Houston. Twice I rented his New York apartment. I took it as an auspicious sign that the dry cleaner downstairs was called Erudite, the one around the corner Faust, and the third one in the area Aphrodite. It gave Richard a kick to phone me and say, "My dear, would you get volume four of Byron's correspondence from the top shelf in the kitchen and mail it to me?"

Of the first twelve editors in this series, now only two remain alive. Just as we were preparing to bring this book to bed, Charles Simic died in January 2023, some five months shy of what would have been his eighty-fifth birthday. Born in Belgrade in 1938, he had dreams and memories that he could draw upon from his early boyhood in battle-torn, Nazi-occupied Yugoslavia.

In *A Fly in the Soup*, his absorbing memoir, Charlie writes: "My family, like so many others, got to see the world for free, thanks to Hitler's wars and Stalin's takeover of East Europe." Simic and his friends played soldiers as the war went on: "A boy a little older than I had disappeared. It turned out that he had slipped out to watch the bombs fall. When the men brought him back, his mother started slapping him hard and yelling she's going to kill him if he ever does that again. I was more frightened of her slaps than of the sound of the bombs." When the Americans arrived in Belgrade, they took the Simic family to the barracks and gave them chewing gum, chocolate, bacon and eggs. "The war ended the day before May 9, 1945, which happened to be my birthday," Simic remarked. At the time he worried: "Now there won't be any more fun." The explanation: "In wartime, there is no parental supervision; the grown-ups are so busy with their lives, the kids can run free."

Maybe the happiest moment in Charlie's life came when he and his family arrived in America in 1954. Charlie and his brother watched a Dodgers–Giants game on television, ate burgers and fries, and ended in a jazz club (the Metropole Café): "I was all absorbed in the music. This was definitely better than any radio. It was heaven." Charlie didn't start writing poetry until he was twenty-one. After serving in the U.S. Army, he attended New York University, graduating in 1966. He became a U.S. citizen in 1971.

Charlie wrote poems in English before he thought to translate the Serbian poetry he had read as a youth. He wondered what his poetry would be like if he wrote in Serbian. How much does the language itself modify what a poem says? To find out, Simic undertook the translations that culminated in *The Horse Has Six Legs: An Anthology of Serbian Poetry* (Graywolf, 1992). The book comprises the work of eighteen modern poets as well as "women's songs" and folk poems. "Translation is an actor's medium," Simic wrote. "If I cannot make myself believe that I'm writing the poem that I'm translating, no degree of aesthetic admiration for the work can help me. Imaginative affinity is what one needs to accomplish the identification and risk the impossible. In a successful translation, one indeed does, at times, become the Other." Branko Miljković is one Serbian poet whose sensibility overlaps with Simic's. Consider his two-line poem "Agon": "While the river banks are quarreling, / The waters flow."

In his poetry Simic raised laconic mystery to an aesthetic ideal. He wrote poems that critics characterized as surreal and he did highly innovative work with the prose poem as a form. History provides the dreamscape. One of the prose poems in *The World Doesn't End* (1989) begins "I am the last Napoleonic soldier. It's almost two hundred years later and I am still retreating from Moscow." When this book of prose poems won the Pulitzer Prize, it marked a signal event in the history of the genre that Baudelaire invented in Paris in the 1860s and had now finally established its legitimacy in the United States. When I worked with Charlie on *The Best American Poetry 1992*, I remember the poems that knocked us out—we were crazy about "Nostalgia" by Billy Collins, then a new voice, for example. After that year of close reading, we would sometimes get together for lunch or dinner in New York. Helene, Charlie's wife, joined us, and we talked as much about mutual friends and crazy university policies, jazz and popular songs, as about poetry. A professor at the University of New Hampshire, Charlie liked coming to the city and did his share of teaching at NYU. He loved the female singers of the 1920s and made me tapes of Lillian Roth ("Tell Me, Why Am I So Romantic?") and Bee Palmer ("Please Don't Talk About Me When I'm Gone") and of great piano music that he recorded in bars. In the background you could hear someone shouting "hey Paulie"—people at the bar holding their conversations, music or no; Charlie got a kick out of that. Wine, he knew his wines, and a favorite New York restaurant of his was Provence on MacDougal Street near where I lived.

"Awe is my religion, and mystery is its church," Simic writes, and this edict, complemented by a keen, sometimes tragic sense of humor, marked the spirit of his poems. Charlie has a poem, "On This Very Street in Belgrade," that in its succinctness and its merger of memory and dream, past and present, is characteristic of its author:

> Your mother carried you
> Out of the smoking ruins of a building
> And set you down on this sidewalk
> Like a doll bundled in burnt rags,
> Where you now stood years later
> Talking to a homeless dog,
> Half-hidden behind a parked car,
> His eyes brimming with hope
> As he inched forward, ready for the worst.

When I visited Charlie in New Hampshire, he introduced me to the music of tenor saxophonist Don Byas: "Body and Soul," "Easy to Love," "Laura." On the way to the airport, I found myself humming "Chattanooga Choo-Choo," and Charlie said he still knew the words by heart. He proceeded to sing it in Serbian.

★★★

Letters, at the home office of *The Best American Poetry* series, we get letters, we get stacks and stacks of letters. Some are more or less routine. To whom shall we send next year's issues? There's a printer's error in my poem. I've changed my address. May we have permission to reprint? Attached are my poems from periodicals since last November.

Plaintiffs write to register their opinions of the latest year's volume. Some relay that this year's book doesn't measure up to last year's in quality. Amid such correspondence it is lovely to receive unsolicited praise from someone who has benefited from *The Best American Poetry*. On the first day of fall I heard from Jane Wong, whose poem "Thaw" was selected by Sherman Alexie for the 2015 volume. "It meant the world to me, and my mom actually saw me read for the very first time at the launch at the New School," she wrote. "It was utterly transformative." In sum, "*BAP* changed my life in such beautiful ways (and I also adore teaching the anthology series!)."

Ken Lauter is one fan who takes the series seriously. He sent me his meditations about *The Best American Poetry* in the form of a seventy-line poem replete with footnotes. With his permission—and in honor of all the other readers out there with strong opinions, I present two segments from Lauter's "Re-Reading the *BAP*s—An Ode." The poem begins with confessions—that, for example, the writer is nothing if not a faithful reader:

> I rush out to buy every new *BAP* on the very day
> it comes out, and immediately gorge myself on it,
> cover to cover, in a kind of delirium of joy, hope,
> envy, disgust, bafflement, and anger—both from
> the poems and the poets' own comments on them,
> which—third confession—I sometimes think are
> crisper and more insightful than the poems!

Lauter sums up the pluses and minus of his experience, pledges "to go on re-reading *BAP*s for as long as I live," and picks out some favorites:

> So there you have it: *BAP*s are both bliss and bane.
> In the '97 issue, for instance, I love Jayne Cortez's
> "The Heavy Headed Dance" more every time
> I read it. Ditto for Margaret Gibson's stunning
> "Black Snake (*BAP 2009*) and John Brehm's fine
> "Intrigue in the Trees" (*BAP 2017*) all of which
> I admit hit my poetic sweet spot: meditations on
> how animals inhabit the world and our minds.

I do not have the space to print the ode in its entirety. Perhaps it will appear in a literary journal open to such meditations.

That poets compete with one another is natural; that there is more blame than praise in the discourse is equally inevitable. I like what Keats wrote when he read hostile reviews of his poems: "Praise or blame has but a momentary effect on the man whose love of beauty in the abstract makes him a severe critic on his own works." Poetry is not a career but a vocation.

ELAINE EQUI was born in Oak Park, Illinois, in 1953. She received an MA in creative writing with an emphasis in poetry from Columbia College in Chicago. She is the author of ten collections of poetry including *Voice-Over*, which was chosen by Thom Gunn for the San Francisco State Poetry Award (1998); *Ripple Effect: New and Selected Poems* (2007); and most recently, *The Intangibles* (2019). A new collection, *Out of the Blank*, is forthcoming from Coffee House Press. Widely published and anthologized, her work is included in *Postmodern American Poetry: A Norton Anthology* as well as six editions of *The Best American Poetry*. "I like the fact that for the most part, my poems are pretty accessible. I don't consciously aim for that, but I do know that my sense of audience is always a mix of literary and non-literary types," she has said. "My work has been informed by a wide range of styles including surrealist, concrete, and classical Chinese poetry, so it's not unsophisticated—just willfully direct in a minimalist sort of way." Equi's writing has been translated into French, Arabic, Spanish, and Croatian. She has taught in many creative writing programs, including those of Columbia College, New York University, City College of New York, and The New School. She lives in New York City.

INTRODUCTION

by Elaine Equi

◇　◇　◇

Poetry, for me, is a spiritual practice. Reading and writing it puts me in touch with something much bigger than myself, something intangible yet quite real. Because poems can be read in the context of other poems, it puts me in touch with the tradition—with writers of the past and also with writers of the present. I know some people have an aversion to the word "spiritual" because it has religious connotations, but the realm of the spirit is vaster than orthodoxies and institutions. Even if you're a total materialist, you can think of spirit as the unknown—an uncharted realm of possibility. In poems, we converse and commune with the zeitgeist or spirit of the age. Another word to substitute for "spirit" might be "silence"—the nourishing interiority from which thoughts and ideas emerge. Or as French philosopher Jean Wahl put it: "Perhaps poetry is only our way of coloring and making vibrate the silence that succeeds us, or which is contemporary with us." Similarly, we can equate spirit with the Buddhist quality of space or emptiness. I'll avoid the word "void," which seems to imply a lack, and I think of poetry as the opposite. One of my favorite definitions of poetry is an aphorism by Joe Brainard, evincing his characteristic simplicity and elegance: "Poetry is that certain something we so often find missing." What I like best in this statement is the sense of discovery it points to. You read a poem you love, and it's as if once again you've discovered what poetry means to you. I must admit, I also like the vagueness of a "certain something." You won't know what it is until you find it—and you won't find it unless you look.

For the past year, I've spent a good deal of my time looking for poems. I normally read a lot of poetry, but I haven't read so extensively outside my own comfort zone and interests in a long time. And I don't usually focus exclusively on what's going on right now in American poetry. It's been a tremendously rewarding and exciting experience. As someone who has taught for many years, I'm accustomed to the agrarian model of planting seeds and nurturing slow growth. It's been a delightful change to switch roles and become more of a hunter. In fact, the task became addictive—I couldn't stop looking for poems. It turns out I like "shopping" for poems (to use a less spiritual metaphor) better than I like shopping for gourmet snacks, designer bags, or just about anything else, poetry being the one luxury I can't do without. As Audre Lorde says, "Poetry is not a luxury. It is a vital necessity of our existence." Baudelaire is even more emphatic, insisting "You can live three days without bread—without poetry, never."

A great perk of editing *Best American Poetry* is that it comes with a lot of magazine subscriptions. I started to look forward to the mail again, which instead of mostly bills and flyers, brought a steady stream of interesting publications my way. Even so, I worried that there was a lot I wasn't seeing. I began scouring bookstores, both chains and indie ones. Some do better than others at stocking a small selection of poetry magazines, but not surprisingly, literary journals are not a high priority, especially since the decline of print. Of course, I looked online, too. I already knew of many cool digital magazines and found a lot more by constantly refining my searches. Among my biggest allies were people who shared their recently published poems, along with links to the site on Facebook, Instagram, and Twitter. Whatever you may think of social media, there's a wonderful quickness to the way it allows us to sample a wide variety of magazines we might otherwise be unaware of.

No matter their format, magazines still help define poetry. They are more than just a place to publish—although that alone is a pretty good reason to support them. Often, they also feature commentary, reviews, and essays on the latest aesthetic debates. Magazines are where one discovers the poems people are talking about and why. Publishing a magazine requires a serious commitment and investment of time and resources. The challenge is intense in light of ongoing budget cuts at universities and in nationally funded arts programs. That's why I'd like to encourage everyone reading this, anyone who cares about poetry, to find one or two journals that speak to you and subscribe. Forgive the sales pitch; this is something I feel passionate about. We need to take care of our literary environment, just as we need to take care of our physical environment. You might also consider making a donation to Poetry Daily or the Academy of American Poets' Poem-a-Day, two excellent free services that deliver a poem to your inbox each day. I'm sure many of you are already familiar with them. I was, too, but it was only during the past year that I made a special point of reading them both every day. It became a pleasant ritual that I looked forward to and provided a welcome counterpoint to the sinking feeling that often accompanies scanning the day's headlines. But this anthology is not called Best American Magazines, so now let me get back to the poems.

The idea that I was looking for the "best" created a powerful focal point. I understood best to mean the most engaging, most original, most stimulating work I came across. I didn't overthink it. For my purposes, "best" would be a mutable word, not a canonical one. I wasn't looking for the best poetry of all time. What was best one day might change in a month or two as I continually sifted through a calendar year's worth of literary journals (fall 2021 to fall 2022 to be exact). Perhaps I shouldn't admit to being surprised by how much amazing writing I found. I could easily have filled another volume. But there being only seventy-five slots in this format, I had to make some difficult choices.

Since evaluating poems is such a subjective art, I thought you might want to know a little more about my own taste and poetic proclivities. When I was young, I was a great fan of the playful exuberance and inventiveness of the New York School. Over the years, my enthusiasms widened to include a spectrum of styles and approaches, from the dramatic and performative to the literary and textual—in other words, from stage to page. Having so broad a range of interests, I pride myself on being able to meet a poem on its own terms. That said, like everyone, I do have my preferences.

First and foremost, I'm something of a minimalist, or to adapt the words of Sir Mix-a-Lot: "I like short poems and I cannot lie." This predilection will quickly become apparent as you thumb through the anthology. Far from finding short poems to be too simple or all alike, I'm always intrigued by the wide variety of moods and experiences they capture and the many forms they take. I like haiku, philosophical aphorisms, homey proverbs, fragments, concrete poems, jokes, and more. One could easily say that the short form as practiced by Emily Dickinson, William Carlos Williams, Langston Hughes, Lorine Niedecker, Robert Creeley, and others is as much at the heart of American poetry as the long, encyclopedic lists of Whitman and Ginsberg.

I like the immediacy of short poems, as well as the way they frame and foreground words. Short poems work hard because they have to. The restriction of the form produces innovation. Take, for example, "Three Shrimp Boats on the Horizon" by Japanese poet/translator Miho Kinnas, which I will quote here in its entirety.

Moon.	White.	Seagulls.
Kites.	Cirrus.	Horizon.
Air.	Water.	Wishes.
Turn.	Wait.	Listen.
Shades.	Mirrors.	Distance.
Depth.	Tones.	Whispers.
Prussian.	Blues.	Strings.
Cries.	Lost.	Crystal.
Rock.	Paper.	Scissors.

Here's a poem that can be read horizontally, vertically, in three-word stanzas, even diagonally. I'm struck by the use of periods. We are greeted with a collection of one-word sentences. Each word is a discrete unit; as a result, the words point not only to each other but to themselves. My takeaway: these are building blocks with which we can construct our own meanings. The poem describes a beautiful landscape—but not a static one—rather one that is continually remade and remixed by the reader. The interactive, playful quality is underscored by the last line alluding to the game: rock, paper, scissors.

Charles Bernstein's, "Shorter Russian Poem" calls up a whole world of emotions in the space of twelve very short lines.

> famine, plague
> floods, rains
> droughts
> poverty, robberies
> kidnappings
> civil war
> invasions
> tyrannies upon
> tyrannies
> . . . and then
> the dark times
> came

The first part of the description leads you to assume that you're getting the whole picture, but then the shift at the end shows you've assumed too much—that the catastrophe has only just begun. Such abrupt turns are what jokes are made of, but this is a joke that dares you to laugh. The mix of humor and horror is reminiscent of those times when you hear news so extravagantly or improbably terrible that your anxiety escapes in the form of an involuntary laugh, a complex emotional response consistent with the sense of fear and confusion we all felt when we heard about the war in the Ukraine.

I am inordinately fond of the list poem. List poems can be any length, but we associate them with long poems, like those of Walt Whitman. The impulse to list is generally a good strategy not only for enumerating specific qualities, but also as a way to amplify, enhance, or embellish an idea. A list can define or limit, but it is more often an invitation to extend a subject. We come into contact with more lists than menus, which are themselves lists. We have to-do lists; bucket lists; lists of the best movies, songs, restaurants, and most influential people. Lists are in our DNA, itself a catalog of chromosomes and characteristics. If iambic pentameter was said to mimic the heartbeat—or was it the hoofbeat of the horses poets once rode?—lists are the perfect form for multitasking selves in an information age.

There are several excellent list poems included here. I would undoubtedly have added more except that my love of lists was sublimated into the larger project of making my own list of poems for this anthology. I was especially delighted when David Lehman and I began working together and he put me in charge of keeping "the list" (that's actually what we called it) and sending him updated versions as we went along.

Behind every good list poem is a cool concept—one that gives the structure and cohesion that transforms a list into a poem. Sometimes I like to think of a list poem as a list of ingredients, but unlike those we see on products, the poem's ingredients help us see the object or idea they describe in a daringly fresh way. For example, in "Fortune," Rae Armantrout uses a childhood memory of shopping for fabric with her mother to launch into a list of micro-meditations on contemporary colors. David Trinidad's Wikipedia cento, "The Poems Attributed to Him May Be by Different Poets," constructs the portrait of an ideal classical poet by collecting biographical facts from the lives of many poets in the *Greek Anthology*. And then there is the poem "Places with Terrible Wi-Fi" by J. Estanislao Lopez. By listing places where Wi-Fi is not, the poem suggests that as pervasive as our technology is today, there are parts of our imaginative and mundane lives that it cannot reach. At the same time, this strange technology, invisible to us, does indeed seem as mysterious as many of the mystical locations in the poem, including "The figurative abyss. The literal heavens. . . . My favorite cemetery, where I can touch the white noise distorting memory."

Two other qualities I deeply appreciate in poems are humor and wit. Of course, not all poems need to be funny, not all subjects lend themselves to humor, but a great many serious ones surprisingly do. I've always liked funny poems, but during the pandemic, finding things that would make us laugh seemed more essential than ever—practically a survival skill. As Mattheus Delius, a Renaissance writer on humor put it, "A joke is great wisdom, and a joke sometimes outwits severity." More than simply entertaining us, humor, satire, and irony in poetry help us meet life's challenges and absurdities. Such qualities also offer effective tools for social critique, allowing us to approach difficult topics without becoming too defensive. Poems that are witty enjoy the permission accorded to the fool in Shakespeare. Humor offers a mask through which they can tell the truth. Take these lines from Lee Ann Brown's "That's American." They display the rhythm of a stand-up comic, but their satiric edge is unmistakable.

> That's American where you can actually eat the fungal network
> Where you can either have it delivered
> Or be the delivery service
> Or go into unpaid labor
> And have to go back to work the next week
> That's American—look at those clouds
> When we learn from each other without even meaning to

In many spiritual traditions there is the notion of crazy wisdom— outrageous and unexpected utterances designed to short-circuit our usual thought patterns. One of the reasons I read poems is precisely to be jolted awake by such "crazy" talk. As the German Romantic poet Novalis writes: "Poetry heals the wounds inflicted by reason." I know people often read bestsellers, murder mysteries, and celebrity biographies to escape. I do that, too, but I also read poetry to escape—not to escape what's going on in the world, but to escape conventional ways of looking at it. I love how in poetry you can encounter statements that you would never otherwise come across, unthinkable often hilarious things that expand our idea of what can and cannot be expressed. Consider these curious lines from Shelley Jackson's "Best Original Enigma in Verse." Are they not a striking way to suggest a social landscape?

> It was the morning, and it was putting on airs
> like a derby with a white geranium in its band.
> The gentleman was in his handsome marble bath;
> the poorer people were ironing their money,
> having learned how nicely it keeps when it behaves
> like paper.

I feel every deck needs a few wild cards and I made sure to include some in this anthology. They are a reminder that the spirit of poetry need not be pious.

One thing I noticed in many of the magazines I looked at, large or small, print or digital, was a real effort to be more global in their perspective. I was impressed to see many translations included everywhere, as well as whole issues featuring only poems in translation, or devoted entirely to work by poets of a specific country. While translations are not eligible for inclusion in *The Best American Poetry*, this movement toward representing more cultural and ethnic diversity allowed me to find numerous exceptional poems written by poets born in other countries who have emigrated to the United States. Included in this anthology are works authored by people originally from Argentina, Ghana, Japan, Iraq, Ukraine, Russia, and Belarus, as well as poems by the children of immigrants from all around the world. These voices enrich this collection immeasurably.

Both of my parents came to America from Italy when they were children in the early part of the twentieth century. I grew up hearing Italian spoken (mostly from my grandparents) as well as English and enjoyed the way the two languages blurred and blended together in my home life. I liked discovering how each language had its own music and temperament, its own curse words and colloquial expressions. During my teenage years, the first poet to have a tremendous influence on me was Lorca by way of the New Directions paperback of his selected poems. I'm sure whole legions of poets sprang up inspired by that book. I think I was attracted not only by the work, but by the fact that it was in translation—that I knew different languages were involved in the making of it. It encouraged me to form the notion of Poetry as a universal language made to cross borders.

At a time of toxic nationalism, it's refreshing that in the world of poetry the tradition of cosmopolitanism remains strong. Lest we forget, the United States is historically a place where people from all over the world could not only find a home but enrich American culture by contributing their creativity. Poetry reminds us of the value and excitement of such cross-cultural collaboration. Like scientists who share ideas through the language of mathematics, poets are relentless in their own willingness to join forces in the pursuit of their art.

It's autumn 2022 and I'm nearly finished with my stint as guest editor. I remember when I began selecting poems, there was a sense of optimism in the air. Spurred on by greater numbers of people being vaccinated, and more places gradually and cautiously reopening, it seemed as if regarding the pandemic, we were turning a corner. Even though it was only November, people began talking about New Year's Eve and what a pleasure it would be to bid farewell to what had been yet another extraordinarily taxing year. Yet simultaneously with making holiday plans, the case numbers of people with Omicron, the latest variant, began to surge. Like many of my friends in New York, my husband and I rang in 2022 at home, both of us sick with Covid. It was one of those moments where collectively we all couldn't wait to move forward. But then something comes along and says, "Not so fast."

More somber notes followed. Russia invaded Ukraine and a full-blown war commenced. Closer to home, another round of mass shootings erupted in different parts of the country. Then, a few months later came the shocking news that *Roe v. Wade* was overturned. Our initial mood of high hopes for the new year quickly began to fade.

I know every age has its moments of crises—its reasons for hope and despair and writers who respond to them. This anthology is no different. Some of these poems deal with mortality, aging, loss, grief, racism, injustice, feminism, identity, war, and extinction. Other poems offer prayers, praise of beauty, musings on space travel and technology, as well as celebrations of love, birth, and other new beginnings. And, as I mentioned earlier, I've made sure to include poems that are inspired by the absurdities and even goofiness of our current culture and everyday life. The intelligence, emotional honesty, and originality of these poets have inspired me, and I'm hopeful they will inspire you, too, as you face your own unique set of challenges.

Every year since it began in 1988 with John Ashbery as its first guest editor, I've looked forward to *The Best American Poetry*. As a reader, I know it's a great place to discover a new poet or magazine. As a teacher, I've used it many times in the classroom to spark discussions, and since there are usually a wide variety of forms represented, it's also a wonderful source of prompts and possibilities. Plus, it's always interesting to get each editor's take on the previous year. Past guest editors have included luminaries as distinctive in their poetic vision as Robert Creeley, Rita Dove, Lyn Hejinian, Robert Pinsky, Charles Simic, and Terrance Hayes, to name a few. Thanks to David Lehman's eclectic and truly democratic taste, *The Best American Poetry* continues to surprise us.

I'm deeply grateful to David for entrusting me with this edition. We had a blast collaborating on it. His enthusiasm is contagious; his knowledge of poetry, music, and film—prodigious. And now, I've seen firsthand the tremendous amount of work he does to keep the series coming year after year.

One of the things I find most remarkable about *Best American* is the way it positions poetry in the midst of popular culture without sacrificing the idea of high literary standards of excellence. After all, "best of" formats are familiar to everybody and hopefully appeal to a wide audience. In this way, the anthology establishes a context where fine writing can enjoy a broader appreciation. That's why this book aligns well with my own taste for serious fun, for mixing high and low, the sacred and the mundane. Our collection begins with the music of spectral mathematics and ends with the empty grave of Zsa Zsa Gabor. Along the way, it resurrects a previously unpublished poem by W. H. Auden, as well as a lost poem of Jesus. What other anthology can offer you that?

THE
BEST
AMERICAN
POETRY
2023

The Bluish Mathematics
of Darkness

◇   ◇   ◇

Beyond calculation
beyond known cycles of the Sun
non-measurable
not even a tenth of a billionth of a billionth subdivided beyond the dawns
its own space then Sable colored space that implies orb colored citron that
post-exists & vice versa culled from the bluish mathematics of darkness

alive
as subdivided singularity
as exponential brilliance
a relay of ignition
as visible ray
as birds in untold advance of themselves
as fleeting motions flying beneath seeming waters on Titan
partially irradiated nuclei
beyond the farthest aural galaxies
slipping beyond totalic Kelvin walls
far in advance of trans-Neptunian theology

from *New American Writing*

MICHAEL ANANIA

Covering Stan Getz

◇ ◇ ◇

a line in time, time
curved, held and bent;

we struggle with
the moment as though

it were a shell we
could pry open

with our finger-
nails, releasing

something bright,
soft and pliant,

the air quick
and filled with it

from *The Café Review*

Fortune

◇　◇　◇

1

It could have started like this.
My mother took me to fabric shops when I was a kid.
I would wander through the tall bolts dazed, reading
fortunes in the colors.

2

White
papier-mâché
of the mock-orange flower
on its many stems.

Lavender, as an afterthought, necrotic—
carried interest.

Ocher
like sunset in L.A.,
like dehydration.

The popular mauve-gray
which blends
indifference with innocence.

3

One is chosen
above her sisters.

One tells a troll
to eat his brothers.

An imp gives one
the power to spin
yellow into patronage.

One frills a frill
again and again.
No in order.
No as if.

from *London Review of Books*

"We get the Dialectic fairly well"

◊ ◊ ◊

We get the Dialectic fairly well,
How streams descending turn to trees that climb,
That what we are not we shall be in time,
Why some unlikes attract, all likes repel.
But is it up to creatures or their fate
To give the signal when to change a state?

Granted that we might possibly be great
And even be expected to get well
How can we know it is required by fate
As truths are forced on poets by a rhyme?
Ought we to rush upon our lives pell-mell?
Things have to happen at the proper time

And no two lives are keeping the same time,
As we grow old our years accelerate,
The pace of processes inside each cell
Alters profoundly when we feel unwell,
The motions of our protoplasmic slime
Can modify our whole idea of fate.

Nothing is unconditional but fate.
To grumble at it is a waste of time,
To fight it, the unpardonable crime.
Our hopes and fears must not grow out of date,
No region can include itself as well,
To judge our sentence is to live in hell.

Suppose it should turn out, though, that our bell
Has been in fact already rung by fate?
A calm demeanor is all very well
Provided we were listening at the time.
We have a shrewd suspicion we are late,
Our look of rapt attention just a mime,

That we have really come to like our grime,
And do not care, so far as one can tell,
For whom or for how long we are to wait.
Whatever we obey becomes our fate,
What snares the pretty little birds is time,
That what we are, we only are too well.

from *The New York Review of Books*

A Deafening Prayer

◊   ◊   ◊

ignites ionized air

Night's holy grail, night's only prayer

An autonomous prayer careens into auto bardo,
speeds through HOV lanes flowing in the six directions

Chanting a drone prayer, a rune prayer, Rumi's prayer,
to co-pray a cocoon prayer in woodlands
with rings, silent owl wings, and invertebrate things
with ancient stone forces and surfaces
and winding roads to root prayer; dew beads
coat spiderwebs and pop-up mushroom stands
we stand on at dawn while praying,
counting breath, counting mala, counting on goddesses
to paw rosy earth for arising prayer-dust that hides
the dare of prayer, smudging sage and thyme to reveal prayer's
sliding doors, the deals in prayer, impossible to conceal
the stridulating cicada prayer, scratching their shells,
their freedom bells, their undulating prayers

The murmuration of prayer flight crossing the empty, responsive prayer night

Wind as soul of the newly dead,
its shroud, the foal it rides north-south
to a magnetic center of decay,
the death portal prayer, our one way out

An erosion prayer, the rat's prayer,
the hat prayer one wears to protect from cloudy moods

A prayer for opening or closing eyes. We watch our step
as we tread on the sacred square prayer, the profane
prayer, a Janus prayer rug with a gate to the star spritzing
Milky Way, lapped up by the temple cat that lodges near the root-cellar
prayer, the hate prayer, vote prayer, votive prayer, a passing prayer,
flying prayer, snow flurry prayer, a furry prayer

Listen for the tiny prayer,
one that flashes light,
the blinding prayer, the binding prayer
Our first prayer, the prayer before we learned to speak,
prayers etched on papyrus, parchment, on imprisoned flesh,
toilet paper prayers, crying prayers, dying prayers,
poppy fields of prayer, each prayer strapped
to song, birthed from wind

The rhizome pied prayer that unselves prayers
to molting feathers, father and mother prayer,
funeral pyre prayer releasing
prayer cares, a Gordian Knot deus ex machina prayer,
a common prayer, a humming
prayer, a buzzing, pollinating pod
prayer, a fertilizing prayer broadcasting
everywhere without exception

from *New American Writing*

Three Poems

◊   ◊   ◊

Pathetic Fallacy

Never mind there's
no hole so deep
you don't get banged
when you hit
bottom, or that
the zombies have
overtaken the Capitol—
I still hear nightingale songs
every time I see pigeons
nosediving in early
morning hale, whose
icy spitballs remind me
of paradise.

Rye Sense of Humor

you don't have to be Jewish
to send a salami
to your boy in the navy

Shorter Russian Poem

famine, plague
floods, rains
droughts
poverty, robberies

kidnappings
civil war
invasions
tyrannies upon
tyrannies
. . . and then
the dark times
came

from *The Brooklyn Rail*

MARK BIBBINS

from 13th Balloon

◇　◇　◇

One afternoon you fixed me

lunch in your tiny apartment

　　　cream of mushroom soup

　　　from a can

　　　and English muffins

As you set our bowls

on a blanket

on the floor because you didn't

　　　own a table

you put on

a bad British accent and said

We're having crumpets

It was raining but there was

an abundance of light

coming somehow from a source

outside we couldn't see

From here that light feels like

what music sounds like

just before the record skips

from *The New York Times Magazine*

That's American

◇　◇　◇

The place where Helen's tears grow in fields
Under electricity towers
The way we are always having to run speed tests
That's American where you could get shot for crossing
Out a word
In the land of the free and the home of the knave
That's American where you can actually eat the fungal network
Where you can either have it delivered
Or be the delivery service
Or go into unpaid labor
And have to go back to work the next week
That's American—look at those clouds
When we learn from each other without even meaning to
That's the American persona living in a mobile home
Down the road from the store
There's a wild cat living in the grass that's American
And invasive at the same time
That crawls on hands and knees through glittering piles of glitter
That will never go away even in a million years
They just keep making more of it that's American
Shiny and undulating sea to shining sea
Indulgent thus thinking herself free
From responsibility
That's American how that works
That's American Airlines
Packing people in like sardines
That's American pie you and I

It's so American to roast marshmallows
Made of chemicals
American-made cars make a strange sound when crushed at the dump
But at least they'll pay you 300 dollars

from *The Brooklyn Rail*

Antediluvian

◊　◊　◊

Before, inside was a condition. Pardon me, conditional—before I purchased an armful of objects which would soon become a vanitas on my counter: parched lilies arching their backs like "Appalachian Spring," delicate pyramid of Black Missions rotting to death: one beheaded and seeping carnage onto the marble. This is how I tell time. Overripe. Half-past soon. Before, I was agoraphobic: contemplating whether or not to keep my standing appointment with the hypnotist. I thought she could dig me out of it. I see her veined hand in my sleep, helixing. Pardon me—I've been staring through the window: watching the wind fret the grass, watching the wind. I feel guilty. I take pre-packaged communion in front of the television. I meant ecophobic. I lied, I don't sleep. I neglected to keep my standing. I let the sun blur me into chromatic aberration—fig guts, Delft blue. I meant physicist. I meant inside is atemporal. I meant, before, inside was a persimmon, permission. I thought she could fig me out. I thought she could discover me. Forgive me.

from *Bennington Review*

Yes,

◇ ◇ ◇

hope,
     despite your
crazy schedule

        we
remain
friends somehow.

Hope—ceiling
above the roof
        of my head.

Or spotless

mirror
showing
my
age (I can handle it
sometimes).

Yes,
esperanza.

Speech of
        birds, script
of tongues

across the sky.
Clouds

im-
perfect-
ly snagged
        in branches

                where
some leaves
stay put

while most clap.

from *The Brooklyn Rail*

The Shape of Biddle City

◊ ◊ ◊

Everything is a rectangle in Biddle City. No triangles, no circles, not a one. No swirls, squiggles. For example, this poem is a rectangle, and outside *this* rectangle is a bigger rectangle. Inside that rectangular room are other four-sided shapes—windows, computers, televisions, floor rugs. Even the lamps are rectangular cuboids. This is not the City of Angels, but the City of Angles, boxy, wingless. No building higher than the capitol, no person higher than the next person, everyone remains at a level height. Even the Biddle City accent is flat-backed and angular. There's a record store in East Biddle called Flat, Black, and Circular, but that's *East* Biddle. There are small circles as you move east. Today I'm at Fleetwood Diner where I drink a square cup of coffee, rectangular drops dribbling down my chin. A rectangular bus buses by, rectangular light enters through doorways. Rectangular people do not dine near me. I have my own four corners inside which I sit.

from *AGNI*

World's End

◇ ◇ ◇

Will earth stop spinning?
Will there only be hair left?
We are made of war—
it stays in the air, mixed with oxygen, we breathe
it in and deploy it out.
Our birth is easy on us
but hard on everything else.

from *Mississippi Review*

The Songbird Academy

◊ ◊ ◊

butterfly in aspic?
 Or is it amber?
—rude awakening of green
and the tree under which
someone said,
there is little to say.

But in the air,
whispered speech,
noise and celebration—

grief and regret
rush of water and drills
trains slurring through—

Beaded wings sunlit,
daylit, travel upwind,
unsung by night.

And through
 the air a voice:
Another. Another.

Photo Shoot

◊　◊　◊

after Gordon Parks

The camera remembers, leaves a stain
of you that travels without you,
stays around long after you,
and so when the Negro man,
with the accoutrements of his vocation,
the heavy black leather satchel,
his fedora and delightful smile,
speaks the requisite ma'ams and sirs,
you ask for a minute to don
your church frock, with the broad
collar you like, and you thank the Lord
that it is only Monday and the lovely
Sunday 'do has not tattered to ordinary
country living, and you make the line
of your lip, tidy the curve of your
painted brow and practice that holy
smile, that this lasting image, staining
the future, will say, "God and country."

from *Gulf Coast*

The Years

◇   ◇   ◇

All the parties you spent
watching the room
from a balcony
where someone joined you
to smoke then returned.
And how it turns out no one
had the childhood they wanted,
and how they'd tell you this
a little drunk, a little slant
in less time than it took
to finish a cigarette
because sad things
can't be explained.
Behind the glass and inside,
all your friends buzzed.
You could feel the shape
of their voices. You could
tell from their eyes they were
in some other place. 1999
or 2008 or last June.
Of course, it's important
to go to parties. To make
life a dress or a drink
or suede shoes someone wears
in the rain. On the way home,
in the car back, the night sky
played its old tricks. The stars
arranged themselves quietly.

The person you thought of drove
under them. Away from the party,
(just like you) into the years.

from *The New Yorker*

STUART DISCHELL

After the Exhibition

◇   ◇   ◇

They came back to the hotel after one of their best days,
Walking around a city they had come to enjoy. It had been
Raining and their clothes were wet and the room was cold
And he raised the heat and shivered naked under the covers,
While across the room she charged her phone and texted
Her children. The look in her eyes was always beautiful to him,
And he knew he looked at her too much. She told him so.

Warming, he was waiting for her to get up from the desk
With its electric socket even though there was one next
To the bed. Rising she said she felt a little sick, then
Sat in the bathroom posting pictures of paintings they saw
At the exhibition at the museum. Before opening the door,
She took one of herself in the mirror. In a few minutes many friends
Liked it and one fellow commented she looked like a "masterpiece."

from *Birmingham Poetry Review*

Instagram

◇   ◇   ◇

What if I was uttered into existence through the teamwork of cultists
    and not, as I take it, born of a human woman
under standard conditions: songbirds affirmative, war flickering
    apart on television, rhubarb raising its arms up from the patch?

Would I catch any difference between memories implanted
    into me only yesterday, or whenever it was I was
spanked into action, and those I picked up over time like a janitor
    inching his push broom of consciousness into winter in Wisconsin?

Reality, he thinks, has holes in it, and another oozes through
    like spaetzle from a spaetzle maker, little sparrows of dough
canoodling in the pot's hot storm, skimmed up gently
    and tossed in a bowl with butter, cheese, and caramelized onion.

But it is likewise the soil, the wheat, the clay, and the spinning;
    the grass in the mouth of a cow, the secretion; delayed shipments,
sunsets, and rainfall on advertisements; the unprotected labor
    and Christmas bonuses; every substance and action prior to, after, during . . .

Eat, they say. You have been kept too hungry. What is set in front of you
    is. The road was long due to technical issues but together
we will triumph. Photograph your food. Let everyone you know
    know you know now what your meal is; you know now what's real.

from *Plume*

Days at the Races

◇ ◇ ◇

> *"Either he's dead or my watch has stopped."*
> —Groucho Marx

Away they go, with their outlandish names,
saddled with human baggage, desperate wagers—
enough to make a Thoroughbred go lame,
be it a strapping colt or spry old stager.
Away they go, with Monday in the lead,
and Tuesday, Wednesday, Thursday gaining speed.
Friday and Saturday, poor things, are off the bridle,
while Sunday, bless its heart, is simply idle.
Some like to be there—tremble at the crack
of every whip, eat dust, bathe in the lather
and feel the press of flesh. Me? I would rather
keep my distance, make my bets off-track.
Each week I pony up a little dough,
although I seldom win, or place, or even show.

from *Raritan Quarterly*

330 College Avenue

◇　◇　◇

After she dies, your mother moves back
into your childhood home.

Neither of you has lived there for 35 years
but the birdhouse nightlight still lights up
the dark of your childhood bedroom

and in the living room
the tiger flower sofa still blooms.

Here
there is another you:

still a young child,
she dances alone to scratchy records,

while her parents dial the rotary phone or
put away groceries upstairs.

★

The woman who was once your mother
is no longer your mother.

Is there another mother who has always lived in this house?
Has she always been here, digging holes for crocus bulbs
or sorting papers at her desk in the den?

The other mother, the one who never left
your childhood home, was never your mother.

The you who still lives there, the you who still sleeps
with her binoculars under her pillow, she is not you.

As your mother walks by the mirror in your childhood home,
you see yourself within the gold frame.

You are the age she was the minute before she died.
Your glasses reflect clouds in the shape of a word.

It's a language neither of you understands.

★

In the sunlight on a cruise ship on the other side of the Earth,
a mother is wearing a locket she never found a picture to fill.

Or she is sitting in the backyard of your childhood home
smoking a cigarette (though when she was alive she only
smoked in the car in the garage with all the doors open).

In kindergarten, you wrote a picture book called
The Motherness of Mothers.

At 6 years old, you didn't care that "motherness"
was not a real word.

Or a real world. Neither did your mother.

from *South Florida Poetry Journal*

Night Herons

◊ ◊ ◊

all day long you wring yourself out
work virtually
go nowhere
brain exclusively tuned
to end-times music
till twilight arrives
to fold you in blue pleats of evening
a flock of night herons flaps past
across the sky or your mind
it's the same either way
long-closeted thoughts rise with them
winging out from daytime roosts
to forage swamps and wetlands
to nest in groups
black-crowned birds who croak like crows
swoop low over mangroves
the whirr of wings
real or imagined
blurs trivial things
strange times lullabies
declare doom looms
everyone's muzzled
mired in dread
the future's not mutual
it's mute or dead
everybody misses everybody
try to ride it out
as night herons seek

what the sun
will someday summon us to
after endless-seeming exile
a prayer to be spared
I shall be satisfied, when I wake, with thy likeness
a psalm's promise
the night herons keep flying towards
tomorrow's garlands

from *The New Yorker*

Revisionary

◇ ◇ ◇

I've decided to let my inner weather out.
Even in the nerves flashing, some things
   are only shadow.
What's up with that?
My muse bruises me.
Some days I sit hours to be relieved
   by a word.
Today's word is invisible.

I'm putting trouble into place, turning
   toward what is.
Listening to stone translate into silence.
Here is an old rock covered with lichen
   in the mossy forest inside the self.
I like it here when it's green.
This is me evolving.
I'm hanging on. A whisper.
Certain prayers are tied to this ribbon.

How in hell can nature throw clay into art
   into a speaking being into air.
I saw a world that was an afternoon.
This cloud in my hand.
Sky pouring into sky reflecting the absolute
   of the lake.
The flock and its tangle of shadow.

Nearing the end, I could hear a lark.
Its trill fixing itself to my brain.
It seemed a thing becoming a wave.
A thing dissolving into the world
    as I found it.
Illegible. Agrammatical.
To parse the velocity of trusses and stars
    flowering here at the edge.
Calling me.

from *The New York Review of Books*

Other News on Page 24

◇ ◇ ◇

Someone famous will die that day,
My day,
And the newspaper will report:
"More obituaries on page 24."

For the curiosity of some,
the regret of several,
and the grief of a few.

Those few, they matter,
So they have a nice walk
in the Marin headlands
shadowed by a weary and worn mountain
(still green! still fragrant!
with pine and transplanted eucalyptus,
and most important: Still there!),
where I'm proud that the few gather trash,
but drop my ashes downwind,
and remember as I fly away.

from *Tablet*

Strange as the Rules of Grammar

◇　◇　◇

The two or three times I saw Lil Wayne
hanging out at The Praline Connection

in New Orleans he had a mouth full of bling
covered in forkfuls of greens or green beans

or white rice & red beans on a tongue
of strange lucrative grammar

The answer will be that which allows
the best possible future when the plaintiffs come

before the judge or the farmers
before the king it is not that which incurs unrest

The photograph does not belong
to the photographer it belongs to the camera

God jerry-rigs to the backs of a barn owl & a bat
We get a bird's-eye view via the camera

attached to the bat under cover of fur & weather
strange as the rules of grammar

Like the branch of the forest industry
tasked with trimming branches

Strange as the sound of your signature on paper
All the animals unbeknownst to us

communicate using telepathy
The owl films the room wherein

you are reflecting on something
strange as the rules of grammar

Between being grounded & being buried
between being anchored & sinking

You know how they say at the forked tongue
of the crossroads & at the crooked foot of the foothills

nothing you haven't already heard
Strange as the first wound you ever received

The scar is so old others must tell you
how it was made

from *The Paris Review*

All Right

◇   ◇   ◇

Everything's all right   I'm wearing my water buffalo coat
it's 92 degrees, I'm in Water Buffalo, New York,
No that's not right, I'm in Hot Water USA, but everything's all right
Was it DiMaggio hit three doubles for the Cincinnati Reds, not bad for
a dead guy. No, that's not right. He's a dentist, a Seventh-day Adventist
a mentalist, he was sent to head the rescue effort but he got picked off.
The Arno is not always gentle.
The high water mark is at eye level. Paintings rush
downstream. I can tie my shoes with my eyes
closed, with one hand, in the dark, standing on my head.
The nurses are running fevers and the doctors are running away
We're burying canned body parts in the garden. It's almost
first light, we'll be all right.

from *Hanging Loose*

Admonitions, Afternoons

◊   ◊   ◊

Oh, the mattress fallen upon the freeway, releasing its padding,
  and five miles of traffic stalled,
    as before a shrine.

Oh, the stock option and the shitting dog, the milk spilling
  across the kitchen floor, and that troublesome
    meeting at school.

Oh, the skateboarder who sings in the choir, with spider tattoos
  that crawl up his neck, *In Excelsis Deo.*

Oh, the march of final things past the leaning cathedral,
  the blue abyss in the shape of a wineglass
    and—oh—the flower I found.

Oh, the ambient sound of crying and laughter,
  kindness misunderstood as scorn,
    and love that forgives all woe.

Oh, houses that are bruises, where the shadow lingers
  of one who lived there, and that box of photos under the bed,
    in which he was held dear.

Oh, the love that he was missing that he lost again
  and found again, and finally drowned in consternation.

Oh, the necessary step in the wrong direction, oh well
  and oh dear, and don't worry I love you,
    everything's all right.

Oh, the word "Ah!" exclaimed in the woods,
and the leaves beating against a branch
as if to fly, "Oh, no!"

Oh, the mystery number, zero, snuggling up to infinity
with the others of its kind.

from *Allium, A Journal of Poetry & Prose*

Best Original Enigma in Verse

◇   ◇   ◇

It was the morning, and it was putting on airs
like a derby with a white geranium in its band.
The gentleman was in his handsome marble bath;
the poorer people were ironing their money,
having learned how nicely it keeps when it behaves
like paper. The stereoscopes with their fair enigmas
had been abandoned at their stations
by editors now going cross-eyed in the bar
o'er anagrams of *evil*: *veil*, *vile*, *live*,
or, why not, *ilve* or *vlei*, rank bubbles

rising in their beer, and you are handsome
as an antler, creaming in your clothes
while the geese call, up over your head, in the sea air,
to share the rules of the place, that anybody who wants
can take a dirt bath, so long as they don't mind
it up their nose or in their eyes. "So, queen,"
one calls to you—an honorary distinction—
"it's time to set you fine people
an arithmetical puzzler. Here it is:
      "Suppose a body to have fallen.
Suppose a second body begins to fall
in emulation. Suppose the latter
wants to overtake the former. One figure
falling splendidly, solemn and composed
to his reward (a cheese omelette or a beer)
one reaching, rooting, delving through the air.
Angry, proud and insolent, the late-comer
advances, retreats, advances.
      It's Monday in wherever.
Bubbles rise. Fine particles of dirt.
The first body falls like a portrait
of a falling man. The second kicks,
looking for an angle. Which do you prefer, the ambitious
or the entitled one? Does the leader's
repose begin to cloy? Is the competition rigged?
Sure! Yet here they are now, face to face at last, composing
an intimate figure, a double acrostic of body parts.
Now suppose a transposition . . ." But the geese
have moved on, and their last words
are too quiet to reach you
where, for now, you live.

from *Conjunctions*

The Devil's Wife Explains Broken 45s

◊　◊　◊

"There was a time" James Brown sang, and I want to dance. But that causes the devil
to prance upon me, then lash higher his liege around my waist & squeeze me
till my voice box almost shatters. You're a doll, he says, as he smashes our
turntable laughing at the clatter ancient 45 RPMs make as they break treasures
from a lost last century when sweet soul music elevated our scissoring feet
How he hated haloed Afros radiant with pride & that slide away from suffering—
The devil hates Black genius. Made him work harder than hard to render
it witless and dope stung. He hates having to move one iota out of his trifling
comfort zone. Can't I listen to one piece of my heart untarnished by his guile.
Child soul music is now in limbo, and me bruised again, cleaning up those broken 45s,
but

somewhere on the other side of this sad Kingdom
Another woman augurs the audio
& James Brown sings out "There was a time"

for Greg Tate

from *Vox Populi*

I Ask That I Do Not Die

◇   ◇   ◇

—but if I do
I want an open coffin
I am an American poet and therefore open
for business

Owls peck the windows of the 21st century
as if looking for
the board members
of ExxonMobil
who who who who who

Listen
my beloved nothings
your seriousness
will kill you!

But before you die
my doctors
have prescribed happiness

God is a warm brick
or a claw
or the silence that survives
empires

An old woman
in the rain with a pot of mushroom soup
is one of God's
disguises. Her dog
lifts its leg
            another one of God's shenanigans
and pushes its nose
into morning's ribcage

I point my hand
            God *this* and God *that* and
when God has nothing
I still have my hairy hand for a pillow

Put me in an open box
so when God reaches inside my holes
I can still see
how a taxi makes a city more a city
            slippers on my feet, and only half
covered by a sheet,
in a yellow taxi
so as not to seem laid out in state
but in transit

from *Poetry*

A Marvelous Sky

◊   ◊   ◊

I don't need to buy any records but there is a record store
I don't want to play chess but there are still chess shops
I don't really want to pay for anything right now
The sky is blue, the air is warm, and youth is the tenor

Most people are not excited by their lives
But there's something in the air that might give them a lift
The younger they are, the easier it will be
But there is youth enough for everyone today

A side street provides protected solitude
Suddenly music is in my ears again
Music reaches body brain and heart simultaneously
The ones one wants to reach are reached by music

from *Hanging Loose*

Straight, No Chaser

◊ ◊ ◊

In the warm compartment of the 33rd St.
train the quiet catches fire and I light
my mind on thoughts of you and me
on Seventh Avenue where Perry slips

in and Jeeps raced past afternoons
as if on West Street, how any man could
have had me once but you do. Like today

when icy rain paints the Village glass
and I glide down a strip of slick sidewalk
onto Sixth and 9th, a vision of you rising

in me as a landscape of possibility
and though it's freezing and I'm soaked
through it all I still stand there eagerly

on the cement because the gray light
in the winter sky is evening and soon
enough you'll be off and meet me

with your eyes at Journal Square
and later we'll play, two ballers
shadowing each other's moves
this freestyle of loving, our groove.

from *BOMB*

Three Shrimp Boats on the Horizon

◊　◊　◊

Moon.	White.	Seagulls.
Kites.	Cirrus.	Horizon.
Air.	Water.	Wishes.
Turn.	Wait.	Listen.
Shades.	Mirrors.	Distance.
Depth.	Tones.	Whispers.
Prussian.	Blues.	Strings.
Cries.	Lost.	Crystal.
Rock.	Paper.	Scissors.

from *Wet Cement Press Magazine*

[Misread "master craftsman"]

◇   ◇   ◇

Misread "master craftsman" as "nastier craftsman."
"To heck with rigor!" I shouted in a microphone—retort
    broadcast across
    the college green.
Large-featured prof, the hurried type
    that harrows me,
    mastered the toy
    store's revolving door.
Baptise my green sponge Cain. Cain
    wipes regular household
    surfaces. The blue
    sponge, Abel, reserved

for washing dishes, holds sway.
    (Jackie and Lee?) Dis-
    respectful analogies
    anoint domestic day.
Dreamt I drafted a tiny, three-chaptered Jewish book
    about *La Cérémonie*
    starring Isabelle Huppert.
Two spermatozoa commas on the ascending elevator's
    copper annunciation screen.
Tempestuous behavior of daffodils, arranged
    within a fenced rectangle.

Bird-cries befriend me on West 23rd Street without
            knowing who I am,
without caring whether I occupy a single body
            or several. Bird-
            carillons emerge
from multiple bird-bodies, none I've separately
            acknowledged. Reprieve
            from saying hello to each
            individual creature gives
            spring its identity-annulling oomph.

Dreamt a one-legged psychoanalyst took assiduous
            opinionated notes while
            I recounted my
            troubled history.
He divided my psyche into threes. Young woman reads
            Fitzgerald's *The Beautiful*
            and Damned as she
            waits in a flower district
traffic island for the green "walk" sign to push
            her back into ordinary uncertain
            life, beautiful or damned.

from *Harvard Review*

from Autobiography of My Alter Ego

◇ ◇ ◇

Black Virgin Mountain.
                              Yeah, gore, & all
the damn vagaries
                              of war locked inside a song.
Yeah, sometimes one thing
                              leads to another
rainbow, a choker of hippie beads,
                              & I can't
stop hearing Dad's voice
                              almost going there
on "Nature Boy," no struggle
                              trying to hide
behind his eyes. He almost made it,
                              but didn't
know how to leave dirt on the roots.
                              Maybe this
is why I must keep hurt alive,
                              limping inside
some bamboo cage.

★

Lately, I feel how worlds shift.
                              I don't know
how they slip the yoke,
                              but three nights ago
these sappers broke through
                              concertina wire,
their naked bodies greased,
                              as they ran & slung
wild satchel charges.
                              I was tied up in a hut
of clay & thatch, & a nameless
                              army nurse
sat in a corner, sizing me up,
                              camouflaged
in blackface, & she wore
                              next to nothing.
I heard a tap on the other side
                              of the wall,
sounding a message in code,
                              & the nurse Lt.
stood up, & said, John.

                    ★

What's going on here,
                    huh? I mean, look,
the Navy pilot never played
                              blind czar of Id
ransacking the rosebushes
                              on a false trail,
& we need him at our backs.
                              What hellhole
do heel spurs rise from?
                              Pardon my brogue.
All summer the devil
                              was sharping his blade
on cold black whetstone,
                              & now this hard rain

falling inside, turning life

                               into gray moss,

but I still love my jackfruit.

               ★

Sometimes I hear Roberta

                    saying, Lawd,

come here, Boy,

              & let us talk glory days.

We sit there, ruminating,

                  wondering why

police would shoot

               unarmed Black folks,

gazing at our faces

                in the water, as the cork

bobs, & nylon line tightens,

                   my bone hook

in the throat of a gold-belly

                  perch big as two

hands, & I feel the river

               growing angry,

ready to leap the bank,

                ready to rampage

one hundred years in one

                 night, red

dusk to dawn's new season.

from Poem-a-Day

I Meant To

◊ , ◊ ◊

I meant to put those
sixty-three names
and email addresses
in the BCC blind copy
space, not the CC
copy space. I meant to

send it to him, not her.
I meant to swallow not
drool, on the computer,
my lap, your sleeve, my
arm, the floor, that first
edition, in the drawer.

I meant to walk and
move with that feline
grace someone once
said I had, not wobble
and stagger like an
old wino. I meant to

hit the "y" not the "t"
the "h" not the "g"
the "b" not the "v,"
return not send,
amends not amen.
I meant to stand up

straight not bend, to
sit upright not slouch,
to not fall down and
get stuck between the
couch and a hot pipe
that burned my back

like the prolonged
sting of a fierce slap.
I meant to stay twenty-
nine or forty-nine, not
be seventy-nine turn-
ing eighty in May this

way, drooling and
stumbling and un-
able to make a fist
with my right hand
or grasp a utensil in
the proper way but

instead need foam
additions to the
handles for my one
or two fingers that
can still curl without
help. I meant to be

the exception to
obviously aging or
a long gone legend
by now not a bent
over drooling old
man who still often

feels like a woman
inside but I'll accept
what I'm left with for
as long as I can and
still be grateful for all
that I've been and am.

from *The Best American Poetry Blog*

Green Moon

◇   ◇   ◇

Green, how I want you green.
—Lorca

I am sorry I let you down
I was writing this poem
In the middle of everything
The way they wanted it
Spring like a gun to the head
Green how I want you
I'm so sorry flower
I let you down
I was a pink warrior
A violent concoction
Someone mixed me up by accident
But don't be sorry for me
Nothing like a lake
To go admire
As you drive past it
On the way to something
A real miracle
And if you showed up here tonight
Like I wanted you to
I wouldn't stop to apologize
I'd embrace you
Without thinking
How I wanted you then
How I still do

Green like I know you better
If I could do it over again
I wouldn't

from *The Paris Review*

Traces

◇　◇　◇

I know where I was
on this day
in 1967

because I wrote a poem that day
and made 8/8/67 its tail
in the manner of Frank O'Hara

as if poetry were a diary
and you could put anything in a poem
like living alone at age nineteen

reading *The Great Gatsby*
memorizing the last pages
("That's my Middle West")

my job to deliver the mail that summer
in the tenements east of Broadway
where a woman in a nightgown tipped me

and the pale brick buildings
on Cabrini Boulevard beside the Hudson.
I woke up to the sound of the Beatles,

"Strawberry Fields Forever,"
and ate hot dogs with mustard
sauerkraut and a half-sour pickle

at the deli next to the Alpine movie house
though I put none of these things
in "Traces," the poem I wrote

on August 8, 1967,
which ended with "the old plains
of America's darkness."

from *New American Writing*

Hooky

◇ ◇ ◇

We skipped that last class, rolled
joints in my clean apartment close to a bar
called Flowers which we loved and went
to so often that once, Joel's dad found
his maxed-out credit card statement and said,
"Who are you buying all these flowers
for?" That day we weren't bound
for the bar where Fadi kept a back table
for friends and on busy nights let us hover.
It was a rare Brigadoon day when the sun
bared herself in Seattle's U-District and the trees
were in heat and everything felt wild and illicit
and we decided to get as high as we could
and lie down under the cherry trees. I was
straight As and dean's list, but could roll
three perfect joints and even add a filter
thanks to three guys I met in a Spanish hostel.
And when we made it to that kaleidoscopic
row of ancient cherry trees we started laughing
hard and scary-like, contagious and the breeze
was blowing pink cherry blossoms through the air
and everyone we saw was stoned and making
out with someone and it seemed so absurd
that we would ever learn anything from inside
the darkness and soon it wasn't so much funny
anymore but serious. The true and serious beauty
of trees, how it seemed insane that they should
offer this to us, how unworthy we were, bewildered,

how soon we were nearly weeping at their trunks
as they tossed down petal after petal, and we tried
to remember how it felt to receive and notice
the receiving, pink, pink, pink, pink, pink.

from *BOMB*

Places with Terrible Wi-Fi

◇ ◇ ◇

The Garden of Eden. My ancestors' graves. A watermelon field in
Central Texas where my father once slept. Miles of rivers. The waiting
room of a hospital in which a doctor, thin-looking in his coat, shared
mixed results. A den of worms beneath the frozen grass. Jesus's
tomb. The stretches of highway on the long drive home after burial.
The figurative abyss. The literal heavens. The cheap motel room in
which I thought about praying despite my disbelief. What I thought
was a voice was simply a recording playing from another room. The
cluttered attic. Most of the past. The very distant future, where man is
just another stratum in the ground. The tell of Megiddo. The flooded
house and the scorched one. My favorite cemetery, where I can touch
the white noise distorting memory. What is static if not the sound of
the universe's grief? Anywhere static reigns.

from *Bennington Review*

Coffee with Lavender

◊ ◊ ◊

A milky, violet froth
that makes one get out of bed
and climb down dark rickety stairs to the daylight
to drink liquid soap.

Is it my throat that's dirty or my mouth.
Generalities are such dust.
I mean, we are dust.
Accruals of facts are another thing.
The last generality is that we
are all more like each other
than anything else in the cosmos. Probably.

A violet froth encircles the sun.
When I was four my mouth was washed out
and I was purged of worms.
A lot of good that did.

Wormy, dirty, ill in speech
one drinks the essence of a flower.
"Drunk on nectar," wrote ED.

The conglomerate of thoughts
are dust then dirt then a clot
of gray milk in the mouth.

Sweep dried broken lavender with a broom

The mouth being something like a room.

Could poetry circle the sun.

A bloody wheel

purgative in nature.

Purple black knots on stalks

perfume in my mind.

from *Big Other*

Pi-Day

◇　◇　◇

you are an unending
decimal—you see?
no matter how many
b & w paramount movies you see
that are risqué
things will come in
to sweep & vacuum-clean
everywhere
even under the table
cleaning by
a decimal animal
whenever you don't
notice
please let us
stand on a chair
to
give a speech
each of your hairs
says
I am within
the realm
of figuring　　out
how everybody twinkles
　　　　　　　　　　　　on this day
　　　　　　　　　　　　　　　like clouds

thru icicles
ground covered
with snow
how could this be?

how many pies
can we eat?
birthday is pi-day, yay
"you have the pi-day powers"
you know   it's showering
icicles & drops
everything
on
everybody

from *The Café Review*

Moonrise

◊ ◊ ◊

The moon rose in the sky
as the moon rose in the poem
the new held in the lap of the old
and we talked about the weather
and imminent disaster forestalled
since we were together.

Comrades, I am with you
under this very full moon!
and we shall not yet set forth
but will talk about the shape
of things and thereby shape
this hour this day if not
this life—

      Are you depressed?
Does the reflection of bright objects
themselves reflecting brighter
objects' pulsing energies make you cry
your face toward the darkening sky?
Are you too always mooding
the air, sulfurous or snowcleaned,
windwashed, particulated
with microplastics?
I cannot see what I breathe
except when I freeze.

There's a streak on the lake
of a yellowy white you could drown
in for real. Please don't.
All you believers in total immersion
all you who hope yet to surface
I salute you, I on a far shore
but thinking of you as no wind
tears the bare branches away—

There's a stillness and another
        stillness.
There's a whiteness whitening
        the gray.
There's a fullness plain
        as day
in the dawning night,
        an impersonal rock
drawing the waves far away
        to their ebb.
You wanted real things
        food and trucks
and diapers and OK a moon a baby
        says goodnight to.
Good morrow! I haven't given up
        yet! we haven't!
The connectivity is good!
        Today every conversation
found an open channel.

from *London Review of Books*

Tablets VI

◇   ◇   ◇

1

When the sun is absent
the flower misses her
and when the absence grows long
the flower looks inside herself
for another light.

2

My flower will not wither.
It's drawn in my notebook.

3

I am the plural
who walks to you
as a singular one.

4

Urgent artificial tears wanted
for dry eyes.
Natural tears leaked
for centuries
into the rivers
and overflowed.

5

Before you shoot someone
remember their mother's eyes
will follow you wherever you go
until she drowns you in her tears.

6

They didn't like his idea
so they shot him in the head.
From the hole the bullet caused
his idea will reach the world
and unfurl like a climbing plant.

7

Only one heart resides
in each person
but each is a train full of people
who die
when you kill
what you think is one.

8

There's a sun inside each book.
Come and bring the new day
that's waiting for us to open.

9

She asked the night:
Why are you so dark?
Night answered:
*So that the stars' light
reaches you.*

10

She asked the day:
Why don't you light?
Day answered:
Because I became your shadow.

11

Life is beautiful and painful
like a feather pulled
from a wing.

12

When the pistachios ripen
we break their shells
like we do to the hearts
of our lovers.

13

If thieves come to your home
let them take everything
except your dreams.
Keep those in a safe box.

14

She dreams
and her friend completes the dream.
When they separate,
the Earth rotates
slower
and with half dreams.

15

The trees, like us,
resort to their roots
in times of danger.

16

During the pandemic
we are a forest—trees
standing alone together.

17

We watch our days:
a snowman melting away
as he should.

18

There are days we wait for
and they come
and there are days that happen to us
and we cannot avoid.

19

The bubbles in the aquarium
are the fish's notes
about the world.

20

Like a patient teacher
the sun brightens our wrongdoings,
same time
every day.

21

When the bird is prevented
from singing,
his body turns into music,
filling the horizon.

22

The birds never ask
if you are going to heaven
or to hell
and they never divide the sky
into stations.

23

When the birds chirp in your head,
trust their message for you,
especially if they tell you,
for example: *Flying*
is your true home.

24

What if the guns
turn into pencils
in the hands of the soldiers
and they underline
the places on the map
as sites they must see
before they die?

from *Poetry*

Dating Buddha

◇ ◇ ◇

On her date she confronted
  the fundamental problems
  of suffering and death
   and sought a solution.

Effortlessly moving in heaven, she says:

    This is a familiar heaven. But it challenges me. I see a standard
      dictionary definition of
    heaven but can't find God anywhere. Did he go to the bathroom?
      Who made this heaven,
    and what does it mean for this heaven to be real? Does heaven love
      me? Heaven is a bit
    like a river. You can't stop it. But there are no boats in this river.
      The river is constantly
    changing and so am I. Is the river an illusion? The question comes
      up like vomit. These are
    the questions. Live with it. Take some guidance from heaven.
      Take refuge in it again and
    again and again. Take three steps into heaven. First set the river in
      motion. To do this you
    must be very still—stay silly in that very still posture as you
      experience the starting point of
    awakening. You better wake up anyway. You're driving. Keep your
      eyes on the road as you
    creep down the interstate. After all, the highway is very attractive.
      You can't help but get

out and walk through northern India. Eventually I'll bond with
    you and carry on to the
present, and heaven, walking funny comes to the heavenly streams
    of suffering, skipping
onto the path of the institutions of life, literary canons, art classes,
    Silk Road, great vehicle,
tundra, kundalini, power lines it serves, Indonesian echoes, and
    heaven.

from *Marsh Hawk Review*

Chopin in Palma

◇   ◇   ◇

In spite of roses, palms, figs, oranges and three
most famous doctors, the piano has not come.

What is the tempo of patience?

In spite of sky like turquoise, air like heaven, sea
vaulted with lapis lazuli, I have caught cold.

One doctor said I had died. The second that I am dying.
The third that I shall die.

I heard today the piano is in Marseille where it will stay
until Walter Benjamin smokes hashish
and writes of a severe pressure in his diaphragm
that seeks release in humming.

I have bought a McDaniel razor and should like
to cut my throat with it.

What is the tempo of severe pressure?

I can't sleep, only cough.

Is it a tall coffin you see on the horizon? Don't go
to sleep. Play me with the left hand
what the right does not yet know.

Does it matter that I will die before Benjamin is born?

There are no raindrops, cathedrals or fires,
no images of any kind in my music.

Ram didiridi. The mazurkas, as you may know, are respectable.

I should like to talk with Benjamin about *the rush* when listening
is so sensitive it could be cut by a shadow
falling across a page.

How does the weight of C sharp differ from the weight of D flat?

I should like to talk with Yeats about those twenty
minutes *in a crowded London shop,*
an open book and empty cup
on the marble table-top
when his *body of a sudden blazed.*

Is the tempo of empty more modern than the tempo of blaze?

In the middle of a sentence is a seance. There is someone
I have disappointed, someone lonely inside their grin.

I implore you to have my body cut open
so the blaze may not be buried alive.

Come, let us glide along the quayside and read one after another
the names of boats. I will wear my Swedish gloves.
We will drink champagne.

I implore you to go on making that silvery, rustling sound.

We will cough and spoonful, we will open all
the piano's pores and walk through.

from *Harvard Review*

Extraordinary Life of Tadeusz Kościuszko in Several Invoices

◇ ◇ ◇

Coffee was his preferred
bitter bread
of exile.

Back in the country   with large cabbage reserves,
he was little *pan Tado*

                from a thatched house under the doting trees
afraid to drown
in a small pond of shade
pouring from an old ash.

Over time, on his face, pan Tado grew Pan's grotesque mask.

From Paris, he sent an invoice to Thomas Jefferson:
Outstanding balance for American independence.
Remit urgently: Kościuszko Family Cabbage Farm
        Far Far Far Away

"Worthy friend and General," "Son of Liberty,"
Jefferson addressed him in his letters.
He didn't know how to spell Kościuszko's name.

The dotted *I* and crossed double *t*'s of
"remittance"
speckled the pages like specular stone.

Jefferson owed to this military engineer
       with a background in *Brassica oleracea*,
leader of scythemen, author of one polonaise, a Pole
but more like a flying Dutchman,
who popped up on both sides of the Atlantic,
wanted by wars, revolutions, uprisings
named after him, a prison
and his family's cabbage estate
where forget-me-nots speckle the red fescue.

Out of applewood,
Kościuszko carved a tray for his coffee
and wrote to the clatter
of a wooden leg on a never-deserted road:

I beg Mr. Jefferson that in case I should die without will or testament
he should use my money for manumission, with 100 acres of land for each freed man,
instruments, cattle, and education in how to govern.

As a knife takes off through a cabbagehead,
I think of him here,
on the East Coast, on horseback,
scouting these hills, rocks, the rapidity of the local streams.
Indeed, Pan Kościuszko, hooved god of the wild
from a thatched house under the doting trees.

Ladies loved Pan. In Philadelphia,
he drew their portraits, flattering them beyond belief.
He also drew blueprints
fattening General Washington's rosy-cheeked faith
in victory.

Tado cracked cheeky envoys from Krakow:
at this point big honor to eat
body weak English weak
remit honorarium for the fortification of West Point.

And, to his sister:

Anna, You must do better with cabbages.

I try not to think of him here, this
general of the homeless with unpronounceable
names, fortifying
foreign forts, growing
impatient, suspicious, suicidal, never
married, suffering from jaundice, depression,
and from the failure of the regular remittance.

Blue forget-me-nots in the red fescue,
the scornful twinkle of his will.

He was a lonely person among cabbageheads.
He was the only person among cabbageheads.

Now his overcaffeinated heart
is crammed into a bronze urn.

I embrace you a thousand times,
not in the French manner,
but from the bottom of my heart,
Kościuszko wrote to Jefferson from Solothurn, Switzerland,
at a secretary desk with gazelle-like legs,
facing a wall.
In court, Jefferson denied three times
Kościuszko's gift of manumission
("I'm too old for gifts").

A Swiss pathologist undressed
his corpse that used to be addressed
by General Washington   as

". . . Coscu . . . ?"

He was surprised
by its small size
under all those clothes,
so coarse with scars:
scars closed, scars breathing,
ghostly,
gross.

An invoice to self:
out of a corpse
already shockingly scarred
already surprisingly small
they carved out a heart.

The casket with this heartless corpse
was carried by paupers
paid, according to Kościuszko's will
—of which nothing else would be paid accordingly—
one thousand francs each.

A lonely person among cabbageheads.
The only person among cabbageheads.

An invoice to self:
Tado's small heartless body
Tado's bitter sorrowful heart

from *Poetry*

HARRYETTE MULLEN

As I Wander Lonely in the Cloud

◇　◇　◇

Smart machines armed with proprietary algorithms remain attentive to my wishes. They use a little known, mysterious mental faculty to anticipate my urges. Ingenious applications of intelligence solve the problem of desire.

By now, their ability seems less arcane, considering how my aspirations may be formulated to coincide with goods and services of advertisers and providers whose product lines cohabit in the cloud with the history of all my searches as I browse, added to the sum of my mediated sociality.

The cloud's vast, expanding, and indefinite memory stores all the information I create in my interlinked communications, including what I'm writing to you now, as on my couch I multitask in pensive mood, opening my mail to find a discount coupon reminding me that nothing says spring like daffodils.

from *Court Green*

The Facts

◇　◇　◇

The facts sit in an ordinary room. They resemble people: stubborn and without imagination.

The facts begin to chatter. Better days coming, better days coming. They arrange themselves in the shape of a lie.

They're cheating: they only work in the past tense.

They fake objectivity. They decide unanimously.

For example, what do you call that white pointed cylinder generated by the roof on freezing days?

Hang-ice? I say.

Facts say wrong.

The facts await their moment.

In my early years, I didn't think meadows came at a cost. There are no turnstiles or box offices at the edges of a meadow.

The facts told me different. They used the word *property*. And I resented them!

Handle them: they have an activating feel.

The facts dispose like people.

They can mute us. And we can mute them.

from *The Paris Review*

from The Feeling Sonnets

◇   ◇   ◇

15.

If Erato is the muse of poetry, who is the muse of music.

No muse is the muse of music. Any muse is the muse of music.

A muse is she musing about her meaning with music.

Take meaning away from musing and all that remains is music.

It is the music that makes for feeling and not the meaning.

Music is moving but meaning, merely amusing.

We do not mean meaning, we mean the feeling of meaning.

It is the feeling of moving and being moved. Therefore we mean to
mean meaning but we mean music.

Music names names. We assume it has meaning.

It does not mean to. It means because it names but it does not mean it.

I feel my name being called in its omen, amen, and moan. You yours.

It may be the same omen, amen, and moan. The name is not the same.

Is there a ruse in the music. How does it choose us. We are all hearing.

We are hearing. Hearing. We are not hearing. We are here.

25.

Different states.

She states. He states.

She states states. She states her states.

States she his states. He her states. She states he states.

Are they. In the state of stating. In the state of stating states.

They are in the state of stating states of stating. Develop.

Lop. Do states stay. Stay and be stated. Stay, state!

If you state you separate. Are separate states same states. You see.

They are at sea. At sea unseeingly. And or unceasingly. They do not stay.

How bitter it is at sea. Bitter the sea. Is my bitter your bitter.

She states her bitter is better. By a bit. But better.

He is bitter. A state is a state. They are.

They are different states. How different. State.

Separate. To state is to separate. Stay unstated.

United states.

27.

What are these numbers.

They are very odd.

Are they the music of division. Is it long division.

Will there be a remainder.

What is first, number or feeling.

First is an ordinal. It is a number.

An ordinal number tells a thing's place in an order. To tell is to order.

What orders what, number or feeling. Why does this matter.

I want the feeling to be my feeling. I don't want it playing a number on me.

Numbers are the music of taking. To number is to take. Nehmen.

They are the music of naming. Face the music.

Naming is framing. Framing is claiming. It is gaming and gaining.

Book 'em, he's playing the numbers.

Book 'em, he's playing the numbers. He's pulling a number on us.

from *The American Poetry Review*

YUKO OTOMO

Sunday Cave

◇   ◇   ◇

to avoid
the world

I opt out
to be indoors
in the afternoon
shade of the day

a misanthropic hermit
in a modern cave

of the day
of the sun

I listen
to Satie's Lent
again & again

small candles lit
in the corner
of the room sit as if
they were musical notes

from *The Café Review*

MAUREEN OWEN

In space   surface tension will force a small blob of liquid   to form a sphere

◊   ◊   ◊

O went   stiff tulle
rhythms gone haywire
Cicadas twilling timber   beetles
at the grapevine   sultry   chewing
an almost violence in these clouds

a witness goes missing
    translucent as a porcelain
with binoculars on the future   in
her hand

Eyesight failing
her independence casts a spell
as she needs me read her B of A statement
questioning every entry   & forgetting
questions me again on same   I repeat
addition subtraction final balance date
a layer cake of confirmation
her balance after each check signed
She worries will there be funds enough
health ins medicare prescription pills
utilities for her cabin home in Truckee   where
only Holy water rising   Holy   Holy Holy water rising
no one is living now

from *Three Fold*

86

Film Theory

◇   ◇   ◇

A character I love dies and I am ruined.

Things that haven't happened hurt me considerably.

Hurt me considerably, and I'll act like nothing happened.

Nothing happened, but I expired on the cellular level.

Cell death corresponds to an intangible loss.

Intangible loss is fiction's cornerstone.

I corner fiction for a confession: *I'm not real! None of this is.*

Fiction cannot unplant an image, it can only corrupt it.

Film corrupts an image at 24 frames per second.

When an image corrupts a body, we call this character.

A character wears a body, not the other way around.

A body wears shame, its own or a director's.

Anything that contradicts a director, they cut.

A cut is a place where I have been severed from myself.

A character is a version severed from itself.

A version deceased withers on its person.

from *BOMB*

KATHA POLLITT

Brown Furniture

◇   ◇   ◇

Don't throw out that old chair!
Someone said yes there,
listened to Brahms while it rained,
fell asleep over *Das Kapital*,
told a small child about King Alfred and the cakes.

Don't be fooled by the dining table,
discreetly silent under its green cloth.
Momentous events occurred there,
all of which it remembers perfectly.
A terrible silence was broken over cake,
and three aunts sang a song about Romania.
Not your aunts? Not important. They were there.

Your living room's still making history.
All night the sofa
gossips with the Turkish carpet,
which boasts to the glass-fronted bookcase
about the fantastic voyages of its youth.

These things remember so that we can forget.
Who will love the old
if not the old?

from The New Yorker

Poem No. 2:
My Kind of Feminism

◊   ◊   ◊

Like a car that wouldn't go, I
woke up in life to find
parts missing. Parts of the spirit,
introverted body members,
aspects in the soul.
And yokes.
Management was altogether important,
obviously,
not only stopping and going.

Unlike a car missing parts,
I could do both of these.
But the hours or hows got lost
in a maze of wills and obsessions,
bearings and needs.
Clear paths changed into detours and
wanderings into compass points of
lost and found. Echoes, called memories
became indivisible alpha and omega murmurs
in my soul.
My living, exfoliating,
like a black multifoliate rose.

from *Poetry*

Something I've Not Bought

◊   ◊   ◊

after W. S. Merwin

Something I've not bought
is following me.
I see it in my Facebook feed,
peeking out from the top of my email stream—
the stream they promised they'd never sell
owned by a company I don't know well.

Something I've not bought
is following me,
seeing as I've not bought it
again and again.
I see the tracks of its ads
like tears running down my screens.

In the morning, it's there on my phone
before breakfast.
It seems to pop out of the void
in a banner over my browser.
I shrug off its warnings,
tapping a grey tab
that says "close."

In the evening, before bed,
it knows I've spent a whole day
not buying it

again and again.
Not being a person,
it doesn't take it personally.

But if I ever click on it,
I'll never be rid of it.
It will inhabit the very soul
of my machine,
demanding ransom
unless I pay
or exorcise it through
a search and destroy mission
in my applications file.

If I shrug it off,
I know it will be ok—
a stranger waving at me
from an ocean liner
I pretend not to see.

from *Allium, A Journal of Poetry & Prose*

Dramaturgy

◇   ◇   ◇

I'm writing a play about a Kommandant at Auschwitz
who recognizes one of the Jewish prisoners
as a famous poet, and as the Kommandant
has poetic aspirations himself, he pulls the prisoner
away from the work detail to receive poetry lessons
from the celebrated Jewish writer. The bulk of the play
is their discussions of poetry, which the poet
is initially reluctant to have, the power differential
being so stark, and though he flatters the Kommandant
at first, when he begins to see his Nazi pupil's
true devotion to the art, as well as his untrained
and untapped talent, he goes to work in earnest,
and at times they are both simply lovers
of the German language, though the truth of their
situation often interrupts. In the last act,
the Kommandant is on trial for his crimes,
and in the days before he is to be executed,
he begs the poet to publish his work under his own name—
the Nazi's writing under the Jew's name—
because as a Nazi, he feels his own name is disgraced,
but he believes so strongly in poetry, that it matters
more to him that his work survive, than that anyone
know it was his work. The play is pulled entirely
from my imagination, a careful re-reading
of Simon Wiesenthal's *The Sunflower*, and the poetic ideas
of Rilke and Goethe with a smattering of Nietzsche.

In readings of the play, the Kommandant
has seemed more noble than I had intended—in many ways,
more noble than the Jew, because the Jew is suffering
by no fault of his own, while the Kommandant is tortured
by conscience, and driven by a sense of poetic calling
that separates him from the Germans around him.
On the morning of the third workshop reading, I watched
a video of two Russians on an ice dancing reality show
performing as Jews in Auschwitz. I was sickened,
even though I couldn't follow the pantomimed action,
and I wondered if I was producing holocaust kitsch myself,
if my work was as disgusting as theirs, though I knew
if I asked any of my team, they would reassure me
that I am doing important work that rises to the level
of art. Last night, during a break in the workshop of the play,
I told the story of how my grandmother, upon learning
that her entire family had died in the camps,
had burned the photo albums of everyone she had loved.
I have told that story many, many times,
without feeling much more than regret, or sympathy,
but this time I broke down crying, and I couldn't stop.
Everyone at the table came to comfort me,
and I felt ridiculous, but the only thing I could say was,
"It's time for us to go. This isn't a place we can live anymore."
I left the studio embarrassed, and later that day,
I resigned from the production. I don't think they believed
that I was serious, and they'll expect me to show up
at the next table reading. I won't. The play will go on
though I can have nothing more to do with it.
This morning, after taking a shirt off the hanger,
I looked in the mirror and realized I hadn't put it on.
Without thinking, I had started packing a bag.

December 2016

from *Virginia Quarterly Review* and *Poetry Daily*

TIM SEIBLES

All the Time Blues Villanelle

◊   ◊   ◊

Hard to watch somebody lose their mind
Maybe everybody   should just go get stoned
My father said it happens all the time

I knew a woman   lost her to soul to wine
But who doesn't live with their life on loan?
Shame to watch somebody lose their mind

Don'tchu gotta wonder when people say they're *fine*?
Given what we're given, I guess they actin grown
I think I used to say that   all the time

When my parents died, I coined a little shrine
And thought about all the stuff they used to own
Felt like I was gonna lose my mind

Used to have a friend   who smiled all the time
Then he started sayin he could hear the devil moan
Hate to see a brotha lose his gotdam mind

Doesn't matter how you pull, the hours break the line
Mirror, Mirror on the wall, how come nobody's home?
Broke my soul for real, when my mother lost her mind

Tried to keep my head right, but sanity's a climb
Been workin on the straight face—I guess my cover's blown
My father tried to tell me   all the time

Had one last question, baby, but maybe never mind
After'while, even springtime starts to drone

Hard to see somebody lose their mind
My pop said, "Boy, it happens all the time"

from Poem-a-Day

Little Fugue (State)

◊   ◊   ◊

Far have I wandered not knowing
the names of where,
long have I woven this dress
of human hair, here
I have pitched my tent, here and there,
not knowing my name,
or where, not even the color of my hair
nor why
it tangles so, nor where my comb goes,
nor where my brush,
how far I wandered through underbrush,
into onrush,
nor where my body was, nor what it called
itself, nor the nature
of my calling, nor what my scrawling meant,
not that scrawl then,
nor this scrawl here, nor what a self
could be,
nor what a bee could be, nor breath,
nor poetry,
this dog I've walked and walked
to death.

from *Iterant*

DAVID SHAPIRO

A Lost Poem of Jesus

◇ ◇ ◇

"poems of Jesus"
—E. Pagels

I like to kiss Mary Magdalene on the mouth

And drink wine from her lips

And enter a cave without words

I am the song and the dove

And she is the rain and the question

Oh my students do not ask

Why do I kiss Mary on her lips

But rather

Why do I call myself a door?

An idiot knows the calendar

A wise man drinks wine from her lips

An idiot, I prepared the table for her

Now I prefer the Magdalene above my chief joy.

from *New American Writing*

Only Death Wows Me

◇   ◇   ◇

Okay, a couple of things. Only death wows me.
Mansions, big private yachts, I can appreciate
That stuff but it doesn't wow me. Not even birth,
Because at first nothing is there, then something
Is there—but once it's there it's like it's always
Been there which doesn't wow me. With death
However something is there and then it isn't
But in a weird way it's still there and maybe
Even more than before like when you find
The dead person's false teeth lying around.
You know what else? Steve Jobs's last words
Were wow oh wow because he was so wowed
By death which I can completely understand,
Because as I mentioned only death wows me.

from *The Common*

Green Goddess

◇ ◇ ◇

Who made the salad

Whose tangy vinegar made me wince

Who played pouty Venus to my impudent Caesar

Who taught me to renounce meat

Who flowed forth lubricants

Who performed dark sacraments

Whose tart shrub tangled my tongue

Who with unctuous poses oiled me

Who received my verdant sacrifice

Who, as I reclined panting, poured herself into her dressing

Who lured me to the garden and dragged me into deep greens

Who instructed me on the use of the proper fork

Who inserted an oblong cucumber

Who shredded slender carrot sticks

Whose burning bush consumed the sky god's timbers, shaking his heavens to the rafters

Who roused me in damp chambers, dousing reasonable fires to consume knowledge raw

Who at the crack of the vernal equinox, broke seasoned bread into bite-sized croutons

Who parted beet-red vestments

Who swelled my painted cave-beast proud and pregnant

Who put me in the red-pepper pink

Whose celestial power I would enviously drink

Who succored me when I lay pallid
Who made the salad

from *Court Green*

AMANDA SMELTZ

These Squatting Girls in Black Spandex

◇　◇　◇

These squatting girls in black spandex are trying to turn their gaze inward.
When I crack the Bhagavad Gita, I can't find Downward Dog.

No Downward Dog or Half-Lift, no Crow, no Humble Warrior.
Next pew over, an old woman files her nails. My mother fumes.

Easter at the megachurch. My favorite silk banner is hung.
It's shimmery pink with a purple silhouette of a dying man.

I strap on my leather bra and boots—headed off to Burning Man.
For forty days I writhe and flash and drape myself on scaffolding.

A pastor at his dinner table expounded on gender and sacraments.
Women can no more consecrate than can this block of cheese.

Thereafter I did no more consecrating. A vine grew out of my forehead.
Suckers and buds shot up out of my terrible hands and feet.

A plastic sack bulges with Japanese beetles, each hooked onto the other,
Shimmering jade and blue—but they don't know they're gonna die.

In my house we keep the old gods: shit-talk, candor, clarity.
Now fetch me that branch-tangled ram and *think* about what you've done.

from *Prelude*

102

Various Gloves

◇   ◇   ◇

As if the hand had once been an aerial thing, a bit like a balloon, floating off over the tops of trees, gradually becoming more and more a part of the sky, which, ironically (or maybe simply inconveniently), thins its membrane, which in turn causes it to deflate, lose shape, and land on the table in my entry, not empty, but heavier than air, though lighter than life.

And then there was that glove in the Proust exhibition (Musée Carnavalet, winter 2021)—white kid so finely drawn, the fingers no fatter than cigarettes. *Gant d'homme.* What could such a fragile hand ever have done. And what could it have not. I'm alone in the room, so I stroke the hand of the marble statue beside it because the glove itself is locked under glass.

And yet it's still its own animal, the kid of which it was made, the calf, the suede, still grazing in their fields, gathering in their flocks, and wandering off in their five-fingered way through the mist.

from *Harvard Review*

Wildfire Season

◇ ◇ ◇

The wind stokes flames,
    and they leap across
        the fireline; to the north,

a jagged red and yellow
    ridgeline crackles
        with billowing clouds of smoke.

To the far north, a singer
    stretches walrus bladder .
        and, completing a box drum,

starts to hum; he nods
    as a song takes shape in his hands.
        The smallest

subatomic particles trace
    the birth of the cosmos;
        traces of scorpion venom

will lead to new cures;
    one day they will extract
        heavy metals from the moon.

The spider in a sink
    sips from a droplet of water;
        leafcutter ants

will one day march
across a radioactive forest.
In this wind,

pear trees unfold white blossoms,
shape a song as
time detonates inside of time.

from *Harvard Review*

Listening in Deep Space

◇   ◇   ◇

We've always been out looking for answers,
telling stories about ourselves,
searching for connection, choosing
to send out Stravinsky and whale song
which, in translation, might very well be
our undoing instead of a welcome.

We launch satellites, probes, telescopes
unfolding like origami, navigating
geomagnetic storms, major disruptions.
Rovers with spirit and perseverance
mapping the unknown. We listen
through large arrays adjusted eagerly

to hear the news that we are not alone.
Considering the history at home,
in houses, across continents, oceans,
even in quests armed with good intentions,
what one seeker has done to another—
what will we do when we find each other?

from *Birmingham Poetry Review*

Full Haunt

◊　◊　◊

He just keeps writing *Taiwan*, in pencil
Over and over; and after some time
Ukraine, over and over; no phrases
Let alone a discernable sentence
Maybe that's the way it's supposed to be
Some power wanting it like that: *full haunt*
Possession by proper nouns, at the start
And then later, automatic actions
By the body, linked to other bodies
Near and far; *their* nouns for the day: *full haunt*.
So goes this minimalist theater
Staged by news cycles, acted by pencils
So goes the arms industrial complex
Amassing armies, navies, chintzy lines.

from *Tupelo Quarterly*

The Steeplejack

◇ ◇ ◇

a man in scarlet lets
down a rope as a spider spins a thread
—Marianne Moore

What about the steeplejack malingering
on the spire? Easy to dismiss his low-key
fanfare—just another private rhapsody
above the chapel. Pour him the widest
tablespoon of scotch. He's earned it,
picking briars from the rough bell tower,
a captain perched on the quarterdeck.
Someone tell the seagull sailing around
the lighthouse that work has gone digital.
Our imps spin profits en masse and you
better hope it's never enough. Necessity
and coercion feel like freedom, like we
can live beyond what was unbelievable.
Like we create our own enormity.

from *Marsh Hawk Review*

The Poems Attributed to Him May Be by Different Poets

◇   ◇   ◇

He lived in the time of Alexander the Great, to whose death he alludes.

His extant poems are chiefly about country life and hunting.

He is often described as the father of tragedy.

Only seven of his estimated seventy to ninety plays have survived.

It seems probable that his parents, though poor, were respectable.

The work survives, but seems incomplete.

The *Greek Anthology* contains an epigram which is probably the work of this flatterer.

He was an older contemporary and an alleged lover of Sappho, with whom he may have exchanged poems.

Some of his poems are on literary themes, but most are political.

His report describes accurately the characteristic sequence of earthquake, retreat of the sea, and sudden giant wave.

His widespread popularity inspired countless imitators, which also kept his name alive.

Described by contemporaries as "a terrible fellow to coin strange words."

Scarcely anything is known of his life.

He is associated with the Seven Wonders of the Ancient World, which he described in a poem composed about 140 B.C.

Known for being the first to mention use of the waterwheel in a poem.

More of her work survives than any other ancient Greek woman, with the exception of Sappho.

A crater on the Moon is named in his honor.

A man of taste and elegance, yet deficient in gravity and energy, which prevented his writings acquiring that popularity which they otherwise deserved, and may have been one of the causes of their neglect and loss to us.

The majority of his work that has survived is love songs.

One night in 191 A.D., they kidnapped him and threatened to kill him if he did not stop writing.

His career as a poet probably benefited from the high reputation of his uncle.

All of his works are lost and are only known by their titles through quotes by later authors.

He especially excelled in descriptions dealing with such subjects as flowers and female beauty.

He is not usually ranked among the top tier of Latin poets, but his writing is elegant, he tells a story well, and his polemical passages occasionally attain an unmatchable level of entertaining vitriol.

There is no reason to suppose he ever lived anywhere other than Alexandria.

He had a daughter who found fame as a poet, composing riddles in hexameter verse.

His brother was an epic poet.

Swaggering soldiers, verbose cooks, courtesans, and parasites, all feature in the fragments.

About 550 lines of his poetry survive, although because ancient writers rarely mentioned which poem they were quoting, it is not always certain to which poem the quotes belong.

An epigram on an ageing vine is attributed to him.

Her poem has been deemed important for the glimpse it gives us of a girl's view of her relationship with her mother.

He was apparently, although obscure, well respected.

He spent much of his life in Athens, where he amassed great wealth.

He is known to have written some erotic verses.

Most of his epigrams are in praise of wine, and all of them are jocular.

He seems to have been a poet of some celebrity.

Some ancient scholars believed him to have been an eyewitness to the Trojan War.

He was greatly admired, chiefly, it would seem, for a sort of elegant wit.

Although he became quite famous after his death, he was only able to earn a bare subsistence from his poetry during his lifetime.

Best known for his characteristic tongue-in-cheek style, with which he frequently ridiculed superstition, religious practices, and belief in the paranormal.

The popularity which he enjoyed in his own time is attested by the fact that at his death, although he had filled none of the offices of state, he received the honor of a public funeral.

The most famous of his poems opens "Love is not . . ."

The year of his death is not known.

He typically describes himself not as an active and engaged lover, but as one struck by the beauty of a woman or boy.

A total of fifteen poems are known.

The time he lived is not certain.

He wrote short poems suitable for performance at drinking parties.

She wrote a hymn to Poseidon.

Two other poems, attributed to him at one time or another but no longer thought to be his, are commonly edited with his work.

Although his fame was great during his lifetime, little survives of his poetry today.

A large proportion of his epigrams are directed against doctors.

Her epigrams were inspired by Sappho, whom she claims to rival.

His poems are bitter about his wife to the point of misogyny.

He died in Athens, nearly a hundred years old, but with mental vigor unimpaired, about the year 262 B.C., according to the story, at the moment of his being crowned on stage.

His epigrams are generally rather dull.

Some ambiguity surrounds his name.

He traveled in Greece, Italy and Asia, reciting his poems.

In his hands the dithyramb seems to have been a sort of comic opera, and the music, composed by himself, of a debased character.

Aristotle found cause to quote him.

His existence is unclear.

His entire work is believed to have survived intact for over 2,400 years.

He wrote only about drinking and love.

She probably wrote around 10,000 lines of poetry, of which only about 650 survive.

His fame as a poet rests largely on his ability to present basic human situations with affecting simplicity.

He is the earliest Greek poet who claims explicitly to be writing for future generations.

from *Allium, A Journal of Poetry & Prose*

ANNE WALDMAN

Three Poems from 13 Moons Kora

◊　◊　◊

for Kora Bye-Anaya

Because everything has its origin
And I am going place to place from the origin.
—María Sabina

First Icon

when

you'd

arrived

& burst open

eyes

looked

like

enormous

gaze of compassion

or was it puzzlement?

now gnosis,

notice this?

I said to all who listen in

hesitant

reluctant

strident

world

of

sorrow

how

did

I

land

here?

how

may

I

help?

your

expression

carried waves,

a screen apart

and saw nations

    in you

straddle borders.

"Junio con patio invierno"

the yard is waiting for you
it's somewhat spare but a good size yard
never a garden
it is waiting
you will crawl and crouch on the ground
and maybe it could turn garden when
you come and you will plant *Dahlia pinnata*
and have vegetables
to grow, help feed you
and we can dance with the hose,
have a little swimming pool
like most kids do
the yard is waiting for you
come soon

Kora Dreams Her Crown

Tenterhooks in an experiment
Classroom gone empty
Fateful pandemic
I write "truce" with new second alphabet
Forgetting "truth"
Unseated territory of Ute,
Cheyenne, Arapahoe
How far we go a century
Who reads future weather?
Keep writing from stage left
Do lessons for treatise on sleep
Invite numbers & chance operation
As "seer of calculus," as "topos abuelita"
Perhaps a wrong occasion
But spiraling
They'll be back, *please come back*
The storm knocked power out
We bed down instead in another room
Mexico, estates of the Nahuatl
Stylus and astrolabe
With soft animals, lunar moth, mastodon
Kora Bebe in charge, velvet chaplet

from *Three Fold*

I can see Mars

◊   ◊   ◊

I'm pretty sure
it's Mars

I can see it
a red star

but
a planet

Mars
It's still there!

For days
not a plane

three days
at least

not moving.

Mars is there.

It's really
there.

I've been
watching it

that red
dot is Mars

for days
it stays.

I hear
other people

talk about it
voices

Definitely
MARS.

My birthday
comes and goes

I care more
than I should

I was overdue
at birth

steam
came off

Will Mars
still be there

with its red
glow

in the sky?
That dot.

I must remember
look for Mars

on my birthday
Will I see

a red
dot

in the
sky?

What if I'm
the only alien

on the planet?
What if

I'm really
from Mars?

The last
Martian

gazing
at my

former planet
missing home

looking
up?

from *The Brooklyn Rail*

And What My Species Did

◇　◇　◇

A woman who cries is not essential personnel. Saltwater conducts her to the brink.

The first sign of illness is a dry mouth. My mouth has been dry for XXX days.

Endless as an ocean. Is. Is not.

That was the day I crossed the railroad to buy the fabric for your shirt. That was when I breathed in the open air and all our chambers.

That was the day the birds appeared from everywhere, cedar waxwings a few feet from my hand. I lived in their habitat. You shared my room. I made a delicious soup. It snowed.

Against the crooked imperfection of the word, this happened. We ate carelessly. I stitched this in the lining of your coat. Essential to whom. Essential to me.

It was not the same stream, it was not America, not the same America, not the same twice. Not the same again.

A hundred times, a hundred days, it was not the same. We crossed the tracks from 6 feet down with the ghost dogs and the deer. We floated off and returned.

This is how we sing as the ship goes down, said my species.

This is what my species said.

This is what we did until indifference left us. This is what we did when we were alive. We rationed what was left. It was Tuesday and then it was not.

This is how we thought in the sweet cool wake of what came next.

from *Harper's*

Great Sizzle

◇　◇　◇

Pour me another one, please.
I raked all the leaves in the rain and now I'm sore.

My primal fear involves living in a dark forest
made up of half-sentences and embryonic cabbages.

I was frolicking with my fairy godmother the other night
when we were suddenly seized by a chronic inflammation of unbelief.

The old postage stamps are licked. The eggs are beaten.
I look for redemption in comfort food and the second coming of Elvis.

A line was forming outside the darkened auditorium last night
just as the faithful began to chant, "The worst is yet to come!"

I focus on the flowers in the vase in the living room stinking up the house,
knowing sooner or later our source network will expose our files.

There is no way to get your secret back from the secret-stealer.
The soul is mysterious, they tell me. Put it in front of a camera and it explodes.

from *Biscuit Hill*

Sweepstake

◇　◇　◇

Garlic paper flakes off like dried seconds,
impatient for me to put words on them.
I whirl through February, a dizzy twister.
Not every day is a holiday. You don't say?

A genie rises from the bowl. Smoke signals.
Coffee holds out a brown mitten.
We grind the candle light, smelting ardor.
An aqua tug bullies its cargo upstream.

Plenty to take care of here. Plenty to share.
Trains leave every hour but we stay.
Glinting wires hint at the unseen
guides that keep our act gliding on air.

The river slips from steel into teal satin.
Dusk's push broom comes, sweeping us on.

from *Live Mag!*

Song for Mie Yim

◊   ◊   ◊

This morning they released my head

from the closet where the university

stores last century's computers

lesson books proven wrong

I am told I have become a gas station

in a city powered by electric cars

an overdue library card

You are born

  shoulders

    tears

      clocks

You learn different ways

you are unnecessary

You don't need to memorize them

I have told my head

is being moved

to a better location

being introduced into

warm, welcoming environs

I can sing

as much

as I want

I have been told

this is what

it was like for poets

in an earlier time

Now it is different

I am told

Now it is better

from *The Brooklyn Rail*

Parallel Bars

◊　◊　◊

It gets bad and then it gets worse
And then the bottom falls out
But then it gets better, even great, you think
You're there, but then it goes sour, totally alone, hurting,
But it comes back, new breath, friends again,
It's the best it's been in months,
Really clicking, it's heaven, and then
Just about the time you think it's going to stay heaven,
It gets bad, and then it gets worse, and then
The bottom falls out, will it ever get better? and then
It does, it's even great, you blink an eye
And it goes sour, vicious, destructive,
But it comes back, new breath, friends again,
It's the best it's been in months, really clicking,
It's heaven, and then just about the time
You think it's going to stay heaven

from *The Best American Poetry Blog*

The Empty Grave of Zsa Zsa Gabor

◊　◊　◊

On the radio I heard
that inimitable accent
say *I vant to die*
where I was born,
I remember her
so long ago
appearing on certain
Saturday nights
as I religiously wasted
my youth watching
others embark
the boat of love,
rogues and ingenues
disappeared into
commercial breaks
unravaged then
into buffet light
emerged dazed
with a contentment
I have never felt,
some nights
she stepped
off the gangplank
so gracefully
stumbling a little,

one hand stretched
out to the dashing
purser, the other
holding the million
dollar nickel
of always about
to escape without
becoming a bride,
sometimes clad
in the white fur
attitude of a girl
from the Kremlin
who wouldn't talk
to one untouched
by evil, at others
under a blue hat,
a countess of
what could have been
were I not who I was,
she also appeared
perched amid
the luminous
Hollywood square
of afternoons
pretending not
to know facts
about outer space
or islands or headless
queens, her laughter
a sentient bell,
and never was
she until those last
days in the hospital
allowed to be
alone, then one
afternoon just as
she wished
her soul left
the body we all

desired and returned
to the old land,
wind came looking
but could not find her.

from *A Public Space*

WILL ALEXANDER was born in Los Angeles, California, in 1948. His recent books of poetry include *The Combustion Cycle* (Roof Books, 2021) and *Refractive Africa* (New Directions, 2021), winner of the California Book Award. *The Coming Mental Range*, a collection of essays, was published by Litmus Press in 2022, and a critical study, *On Dar el-Hikma*, is forthcoming. He received a lifetime achievement award from *Big Other* in 2020.

Of "The Bluish Mathematics of Darkness," Alexander writes: "I have long been fascinated with the grammar of alien suns and the living palpitation that remains their resonant anterior condition. My lifelong lingual quest has been my attempt at tapping into this mystery not as answer but by lingual interiority as living experience. For instance, the living mathematics that evince themselves as wasps or volcanoes. We do not create these living grammars but to probe into numeric number that issues from mystery that remains a given. As poet I seek to sup from this well of mystery via means of language that naturally accrues from the imagination."

MICHAEL ANANIA was born in Omaha, Nebraska, in 1939. His recent books include *Heat Lines* (Asphodel/Moyer Bell, 2006), *Continuous Showings* (MadHat Press, 2017), and *Nightsongs & Clamors* (MadHat, 2019). A critical book, *From the Word to the Place: Essays on the Work of Michael Anania* (MadHat, 2022), was edited by Lea Graham.

Of "Covering Stan Getz," Anania writes: "I have a Stan Getz album in my car and listen to it often. One night after driving home with the album on, I wrote a note to myself, 'time curved, held and bent,' thinking of the line of music and Getz's ability to manipulate a note and its musical line. The image of time as a shell was borrowed from Paul Celan."

RAE ARMANTROUT was born in Vallejo, California, in 1947. Her recent books are *Finalists* (Wesleyan University Press, 2022) and *Wobble* (Wesleyan, 2018). Her other books with Wesleyan include *Partly: New and Selected Poems, 2001–2015*, *Just Saying*, *Money Shot*, and *Versed*. In 2010 *Versed* won the Pulitzer Prize for poetry and the National Book Critics Circle Award. Retired from University of California, San Diego, where she was a professor of poetry and poetics, she is the current judge of the Yale Series of Younger Poets.

Of "Fortune," Armantrout writes: "This poem looks at the adult world through the lens of childhood. In the first two parts, childhood memories of visits to fabric stores morph into a meditation on the contemporary uses of color. In the third part, a visit to the harsh world of fairy tales segues (via a trip through 'Rumpelstiltskin') into a look at the world of garment workers."

W. H. AUDEN, who aspired to be "a minor Atlantic Goethe," was born in York, England, in 1907. Educated at Oxford, he emigrated from Britain to America in 1939. His books include *New Year's Letter*, *For the Time Being*, *The Sea and the Mirror*, *The Age of Anxiety*, and *The Shield of Achilles*. With Christopher Isherwood he collaborated on *The Dog Beneath the Skin* and other works. He displayed an extraordinary mastery of forms and poetic strategies, and his prose—as collected in *The Dyer's Hand* and other books—reveals a wide-ranging mind with an insatiable intellectual curiosity. For many years he lived in New York City where he exerted a major influence on the emerging American poets of the time. As judge of the Yale Series of Younger Poets from 1946 until 1958, he chose the first books of John Ashbery, Daniel Hoffman, John Hollander, W. S. Merwin, Joan Murray, Adrienne Rich, and James Wright. Auden died in 1973.

David Lehman writes: " 'We get the Dialectic fairly well' is a broken sestina, lacking the three-line envoi that would fulfill the requirements of the form. Consisting of six six-line stanzas, with rhymes substituted for some of the repeated end-words to make the task even more difficult, the poem demonstrates Auden's skill at reconciling intellectual argument with lyrical imagery. Edward Mendelson, editor of *The Complete Works of W. H. Auden* (Princeton University Press, 2022), notes that the poem was written in late 1940 but was left incomplete and unpublished in the poet's lifetime. Why did Auden abandon the poem? Did he fear it failed to cohere or succeeded only as a verbal exercise? Auden was a severe critic of his own work and disowned some of his best-loved poems."

Mary Jo Salter points out that in this poem "Auden never repeats any of his rhyme-words (for instance: repel, pell-mell, cell, hell, bell, tell). Thus he's worked out a 'dialectic' form a bit like a compass: one point (identical words) is fixed, the other (their rhymes) moves. That this poem should *mean* something, and in fact sound like someone just talking in a poetically heightened way, is extraordinary. That he didn't think the poem good enough to publish as is, is a measure of how high he set the bar—especially in 1940, when he was writing a lot of truly immortal stuff."

Martine Bellen was born in New York City in 1959, where she resides in the borough of Queens. Her most recent poetry collection is *An Anatomy of Curiosity* (MadHat Press, 2023). Her nine other books include *This Amazing Cage of Light: New and Selected Poems* (Spuyten Duyvil, 2015). As a librettist, Bellen has written the text for *Ovidiana*, an opera based on Ovid's *Metamorphoses* (composer, Matthew Greenbaum); has collaborated with David Rosenboom on *AH! Opera No-Opera*; and has written *Moon in the Mirror* (composer, Stephen Dembski) with Zhang Er. She is a contributing editor of *Conjunctions*. Her poetry has been translated into Chinese, German, and Italian. Bellen has received grants from the City Artist Corps and Queens Art Fund, and a New York Foundation for the Arts Fellowship; she has enjoyed a residency from the Rockefeller Foundation at the Bellagio Center in Bellagio, Italy. For more information about Bellen's work, visit her website: www.martinebellen.com.

Bellen writes: "The poem 'A Deafening Prayer' was set in motion on a windy day. An election was in the air, and someone on the airwaves mentioned to vote is to pray. On hearing that, the question arose, *What isn't a prayer?* And I began writing a fragment of a continuous shared prayer, loosed from pray-ers, air mailed throughout space and time, for what better way to send a prayer but enveloped in a poem."

CHARLES BERNSTEIN was born in New York City in 1950. He received the 2019 Bollingen Prize for *Near/Miss* (University of Chicago Press, 2018) and for lifetime achievement in American Poetry. Recent books include *Topsy-Turvy* (Chicago, 2021) and *Pitch of Poetry* (Chicago, 2016).

Of "Three Poems," Bernstein writes: "Newly Unmastered: Socially sourced poems made from 100 percent recycled materials, matured in seasoned oak pitch, charred before filling to impart a piquant, indefinable nuttiness. My poetry is sponsored by the center for avant-garde comedy and stand-up poetry; by the First Church, Poetic License; and by readers like you."

MARK BIBBINS was born in Albany, New York, and now lives in New York City. He is the author of four poetry collections, most recently *13th Balloon* (Copper Canyon Press, 2020), which received the Thom Gunn Award from the Publishing Triangle. His first book, *Sky Lounge* (Graywolf Press, 2003), won a Lambda Literary Award. Bibbins teaches in the graduate writing programs of Columbia University and The New School, where he cofounded *LIT* magazine and currently serves as poetry coordinator, and in NYU's Writers in Florence program.

Bibbins writes: "The 'you' to whom this excerpt and much of my book-length poem *13th Balloon* is addressed is Mark Crast, who died of AIDS in 1992 at the age of twenty-five. I refer to the book as an elegy in pieces. Along with Mark's death, it deals with coming of age as a queer person during the first years of the AIDS epidemic and with my attempts to process these experiences during the years since. The processing continues."

LEE ANN BROWN was born at Johnson Airbase in Saitama, Japan, in 1963, and was raised in Charlotte, North Carolina. She now lives in New York City, where she is the founding editor of Tender Buttons Press, curates poetry happenings at Torn Page, and teaches poetry and literature at St. John's University. Her several books of poetry include *Other Archer* (Presses Universitaires de Rouen, 2015). She was recently the Judith E. Wilson Poetry Fellow at the University of Cambridge and is a visiting faculty member at Naropa University's Jack Kerouac School of Disembodied Poetics.

Brown writes: "I wrote 'That's American' during a poetry workshop led by poet Filip Marinovich originally named 'Queering Poets by Sun Sign' and which he now calls 'Motley.' Filip is wonderful at getting participants to read poetry out loud, and then stop in the middle, to write while under the spell of reading a particular poet's influence. We were reading the Langston Hughes poem 'Let America Be America Again,' which has new resonance in this day and age. I am fascinated by the expansive improvisational nature of the list poem form and its flexibility. With the anchor of anaphora, it's easy to let imaginative connections flow, and let the language refrain help you say things under the surface of playful thinking and cultural critique."

KAMERYN ALEXA CARTER, born in Chicago in 1996, is a black writer working in the fields of poetics and assemblage theory. She is a founding coeditor of *Emergent Literary*, a journal for black and brown artists. Her work has appeared in *68to05*, *Bennington Review*, *Phoebe*, *Torch Literary Arts*, and *Bat City Review*. You can find her online at kamerynalexacarter.com.

Of "Antediluvian," Carter writes: "This poem is one in a series of single-stanza, justified poems I wrote during a period of agoraphobia. During this time, I began to consider the stanza's etymology: 'room,' 'stopping/standing place.' Along these lines, the stanza created a literal domestic space in my work (the kitchen, for example) as well as a syntactical one. I began to ask myself how such a space could be limiting or suffocating, even as it's most often coded as a place of comfort or retreat. I wondered if I could enact this trapped feeling structurally.

"The idea of the stopping place also allowed me to locate the poem in an uncertain temporality. The speaker's sense of time is halted. They can only experience time passing as evidenced by external objects (rotting fruit, wilted flowers). The poem is a meditation on 'before' and in the same token a meditation on apocalypse and its after—what it destroys, limits, what it makes way for."

GUILLERMO FILICE CASTRO is a poet and photographer born in Buenos Aires, Argentina, in 1962. He is the author of the chapbooks *Mixtape for a War* (Seven Kitchens Press, 2018) and *Agua, Fuego* (Finishing Line Press, 2015). He received an E-S-B fellowship from The Poetry Project. Now a U.S. citizen, Castro resides in New Jersey with his husband and two cats.

Of "Yes," Castro writes: "I wrote this poem in the summer of 2021 following the death of my dear sister from Covid. As I sat on my balcony, the beauty of the sky and the small forest abutting my building complex brought me, at times, a great deal of solace. While this piece is, at its core, an exploration of the meaning of hope, it is also an indirect celebration of the place where (and how) much of my work is created: in observance of nature, as if from the deck of a suburban cruise ship, with the occasional squirrel or northern cardinal landing on the railing for a visit."

MARIANNE CHAN was born in Indianapolis in 1988. She grew up in Stuttgart, Germany, and Lansing, Michigan. She is the author of *All Heathens* (Sarabande Books, 2020), which won the 2021 GLCA New Writers Award in Poetry, the 2021 Ohioana Book Award in Poetry, and the 2022 Association for Asian American Studies Book Award in Poetry. She is pursuing a PhD in creative writing and literature at the University of Cincinnati.

Chan writes: " 'The Shape of Biddle City' is a part of a series of prose poems about Biddle City, a surreal and fictional place inspired by my hometown, Lansing, Michigan."

VICTORIA CHANG was born in Detroit, Michigan, in 1970. Her forthcoming book of poems, *With My Back to the World*, will be published in 2024 by Farrar, Straus and Giroux. *The Trees Witness Everything* appeared from Copper Canyon Press in 2022; her nonfiction book, *Dear Memory*, was published by Milkweed Editions, 2021. *OBIT*, published by Copper Canyon in 2020, was named a *New York Times* Notable Book, a *Time* Must-Read Book, and received the *Los Angeles Times* Book Prize, the Anisfield-Wolf Book Award in Poetry, and the PEN/Voelcker Award for Poetry. The recipient of a Guggenheim Fellowship, she lives in Los Angeles and is the acting program chair of

Antioch's low-residency MFA Program. She is the current poetry editor for the *New York Times Magazine*.

Of "World's End," Chang writes: "This poem is written in syllabics and uses W. S. Merwin's poem title. Originally, this poem was written in a Japanese syllabic form called a choka (5-7-5-7-5-7-5-7-7), which can be indefinite, but mine tend to be nine lines. I modified the form while revising the poem, though. I chose to doubly constrain myself because formal constraints often have the opposite effect on my writing process. I was primarily interested in freeing my own mind during the writing process. Someone else's malleable title, along with specific syllable patterns, allowed my writing process to become more unfettered (and fun)."

MAXINE CHERNOFF, born in Chicago in 1952, is the author of seventeen books of poetry and six works of fiction. She is winner of a 2013 National Endowment for the Arts grant in poetry and, with Paul Hoover, the 2009 PEN Translation Award for the *Selected Poems of Friedrich Hölderlin*. In 2016 she was a visiting writer at the American Academy in Rome, and in 2013 she was a guest at Exeter University in England. She is the former chair of creative writing at San Francisco State University and the former coeditor of *Oink!* and *New American Writing*. She has taught or read poetry in the Czech Republic, Russia, Brazil, Scotland, England, Australia, and China. A new and selected volume of her poems, *Light and Clay*, was published by MadHat Press in 2023.

Of "The Songbird Academy," Chernoff writes: "I wanted to write a poem celebrating spring and the way in which, within the tumult of industrial noise and other known and unknown sounds, our ears are tuned for birdsong above the more mundane noise. I pictured birds on their limbs and wires as a kind of academy of music while in reality we know their songs are both instinctive and learned. Our connection to nature in some deep way overrides the human additions to our environments. Our awakening to birdsong is often the beginning of our day. This poem appreciates those facts."

KWAME DAWES was born in Ghana in 1962. He is the author of twenty-two books of poetry and numerous other books of fiction, criticism, and essays. He is Glenna Luschei Editor of *Prairie Schooner* and teaches at the University of Nebraska and the Pacific MFA Program. He is director of the African Poetry Book Fund and artistic director of the Calabash International Literary Festival. Dawes is a Chancellor of the Academy of American Poets and a Fellow of the Royal Society of Literature. His awards include an Emmy, the Forward Poetry Prize, a Guggenheim Fellowship, and the Windham Campbell Prize for Poetry. In 2022 Dawes was awarded the Order of Distinction (Commander Class) by the Government of Jamaica.

Of "Photo Shoot," Dawes writes: "Since the invention of photography, a certain everyday appreciation of the idea of the persistence of our presence in this world beyond our life has become a new kind of practice of legacy. The great photographers of Black life, like Gordon Parks, have given the gift of legacy to thousands, and in so doing, have offered a dogged reminder that we have been here."

ALEX DIMITROV lives in New York.

Of "The Years," Dimitrov writes: "I wrote this poem thinking about my friends. I love parties. I hate that we're all going to die."

STUART DISCHELL was born in Atlantic City, New Jersey, in 1954, and is the author of *Good Hope Road* (Viking, 1993), a National Poetry Series selection; *Evenings & Avenues* (Penguin, 1996); *Dig Safe* (Penguin, 2003); *Backwards Days* (Penguin, 2007); *Standing on Z* (Unicorn Press, 2016); *Children with Enemies* (University of Chicago Press, 2017); and *The Lookout Man* (Chicago, 2022). A recipient of awards from the NEA, the North Carolina Arts Council, the Ledig-Rowohlt Foundation, and the John Simon Guggenheim Foundation, he is a professor in the MFA Program in Creative Writing at the University of North Carolina at Greensboro.

Of "After the Exhibition," Dischell writes: "Most of my poems are 'located,' in the sense that they have settings that keep their speakers or characters grounded in places that can clarify or complicate the situations. I have written poems set in restaurants and war zones, mountain summits and ships at sea, alleyways and boulevards—you get the picture—but what better location is there than the hotel room with its anonymous stage set, its king-size bed proscenium, and two familiar characters at odds with each other at the end of a bad relationship?"

TIMOTHY DONNELLY was born in Providence, Rhode Island, in 1969. He is the author of four books of poetry, including *The Problem of the Many* (Wave Books, 2019); *The Cloud Corporation* (Wave, 2010), winner of the 2012 Kingsley Tufts Poetry Award; and, most recently, *Chariot* (Wave, 2023). He teaches at Columbia University and lives in Brooklyn.

Donnelly writes: "During the pandemic I watched a lot of movies and they often seeped into my writing. I wrote 'Instagram' after rewatching two of my favorite movies from 2020, David Prior's *The Empty Man* and Charlie Kaufman's *I'm Thinking of Ending Things*, both of which feature (spoiler alert) main characters who turn out not to be what, in layperson's terms, we might call 'real people.' I had recently made spaetzle, and the way the dough progressed through the holes of my implement into its new identity as noodle or dumpling (opinions vary) seemed relevant, and then everything did. At what point, and with what kind of assistance or corroboration, does a person become real? Suddenly I seemed to understand why we keep posting on social media pictures of what we eat, which we're often told is what we are—namely, to reinforce a sense of selfhood, to get a clear fix on, and of, one's increasingly oozy reality. The effect, however pleasurable, is as illusory as it is, I venture, short-lived. And what to make of the fact that, from the moment we press 'share,' all these self-making images are handed over to a corporate body 'to host, use, distribute, modify, run, copy, publicly perform or display, translate, and create derivative works of'? For a glimpse of who we are we have to look the other way."

BORIS DRALYUK was born in Odessa, Ukraine, in 1982. He is the author of *My Hollywood and Other Poems* (Paul Dry Books, 2022), editor of *1917: Stories and Poems from the Russian Revolution* (Pushkin Press, 2016), coeditor (with Robert Chandler and Irina Mashinski) of *The Penguin Book of Russian Poetry* (2015), and translator of volumes by Isaac Babel, Andrey Kurkov, Maxim Osipov, Leo Tolstoy, Mikhail Zoshchenko, and other authors.

Of "Days at the Races," Dralyuk writes: " 'Good poets have a weakness for bad puns,' wrote Auden, and sometimes even a weak poet will crack a good one. Punning elicits groans in daily conversation because it hinders direct communication. Puns are disorienting forks in the road for some everyday speakers, but when poets come to such forks, we're tempted to take them, just to see where they lead. One must tread lightly, of course. Many double entendres are pointless detours, dead ends. But others, when pursued smartly and honestly, may lead to richer truths about one's relationship to a given subject—especially if one is, like me, so frequently of two minds about things. 'Days at the Races' departed from its titular pun. The challenge I set for myself was to stay atop the conceit, spurring it forward all the way to the finish line. The rails of my chosen form (a modification of the stanza Alexander Pushkin used for his *Eugene Onegin*, a poem full of wordplay) helped me stay on track, turn after turn. This punning method allowed me to explore and express, if only obliquely, my feelings concerning time, work, and social behavior in what I hope is an entertaining manner. Speaking of entertainment, the epigraph is a line of Groucho's from *A Day at the Races* (1937). In typical Marxian fashion, his quip twists our perspective, stands all standards of measurement on their heads. Like all good poets, the Marx Brothers destabilized the words to which we'd grown accustomed, awakening us, rudely, to their full potential—for laughs, yes, but not just."

JOANNA FUHRMAN, born in 1972 in Brooklyn, is an assistant teaching professor of creative writing at Rutgers University and the author of six books of poetry, most recently *To a New Era* (Hanging Loose Press, 2021). *Data Mind*, a collection of prose poetry about the Internet, is forthcoming from Curbstone/Northwestern University Press in 2024. She started publishing her work with Hanging Loose as a teenager and became a coeditor of the press in 2022.

Of "330 College Avenue," Fuhrman writes: "Around six months after my mother died, I dreamed about my parents moving back into my childhood home. Because it was especially vivid, I wrote some lines about it on my phone's notes app when I woke up. I worked on the idea mainly on my phone while riding the subway, but it didn't feel like a poem yet, so I put it away. A couple of months later, I was visiting my dad in Florida over winter break, and my writing group was going to meet on Zoom; I didn't have anything to bring to the meeting, so I forced myself to finish this poem. I think being in Florida gave me the distance (or closeness) I needed to write it. Because my mom grew up in Miami and died near West Palm, I sent this poem to the *South Florida Poetry Journal*. They accepted it surprisingly quickly and offered a very wise edit for the last line. Since writing it, I have completed most of a new manuscript about my mother and grief and phone booths."

AMY GERSTLER was born in San Diego, California, in 1956. A writer of poetry, fiction, nonfiction, art criticism, journalism and other stuff, she has published thirteen books of poems, a children's book, and several collaborative books with visual artists. *Index of Women*, her most recent book of poems, was published by Penguin Random House in 2021. She is currently working on a musical play with composer/actor/arranger Steve Gunderson. She was guest editor of *The Best American Poetry 2010*.

Of "Night Herons," Gerstler writes: "In my ornithological ignorance, I had not known there were birds in the world called night herons. When I happened to read of their existence, in a nature article on another subject entirely, the birds' name seemed so evocative that I immediately wanted to use it. I imagined a sleek, tall, nocturnal bird, somehow embodying features of evening, lighting silently at dusk on the shore of a lake. Gray blue, perhaps, slim as an egret. Its silhouette in the near dark on stilt-like legs graceful as a dancer's. Bringer of night. At peace in the dark. Harbinger of change. Perhaps because the Covid lockdown felt to me like being trapped in a chaotic night that stretched on for years, this poem, sparked by the name of a bird, filled up with my Covid-confinement longings. Longings, I suppose, for the pandemic to definitively end, for social life to recommence, for the pre-pandemic world that seemed to have been destroyed to return intact. Longing to survive into a brighter future. While writing the poem I looked up habits and characteristics of night herons to see if there were any details I could use, but for some reason didn't pull up any pictures of them till I'd almost finished. Was I surprised to see what they actually look like! There are apparently many sorts of night herons. The vast majority of them look rather squat and stubby. Not the elongated crane-like avians I'd imagined, under whose spell I'd written the poem. (No disrespect intended, herons, you are handsome in your own right, you hunched little wizards.)"

PETER GIZZI's recent books include *Now It's Dark* (Wesleyan University Press, 2020), *Sky Burial: New and Selected Poems* (Carcanet, 2020), and *Archeophonics* (finalist for the National Book Award, Wesleyan, 2016). *Fierce Elegy* is forthcoming from Wesleyan in 2023. He has received fellowships from the Rex Foundation, the Howard Foundation, the Foundation for Contemporary Arts, and the Guggenheim Foundation. He has twice received the Judith E. Wilson Visiting Fellowship in Poetry at the University of Cambridge. In 2018 Wesleyan brought out *In the Air: Essays on the Poetry of Peter Gizzi*. He teaches poetry and poetics in the MFA Program at the University of Massachusetts, Amherst.

HERBERT GOLD was born in Cleveland, Ohio, in 1924. After several of his poems were accepted by literary magazines in his teenage years, he studied philosophy at Columbia University, where he befriended writers who would define the Beat Generation, from Anaïs Nin to Allen Ginsberg. Gold won a Fulbright fellowship and moved to Paris, where he did graduate studies at the Sorbonne and worked on his first novel, *Birth of a Hero*, published in 1951. Since then Gold has written more than thirty books, including the bestsellers *Fathers* and *The Man Who Was Not With It*, and received many awards, including the Sherwood Anderson Award for Fiction, the Commonwealth Club Gold Medal, and the PEN Oakland Josephine Miles Literary Award. He has also taught at the University of California at Berkeley, and at Stanford, Cornell, and Harvard. He has many children and grandchildren and has recently returned to writing poetry.

Of "Other News on Page 24," Gold writes: "At age near ninety-nine, I'm fully aware of mortality. The first hundred years are the hardest, but the second hundred years present their own problems."

TERRANCE HAYES was born in Columbia, South Carolina, in 1971. His recent publications include *American Sonnets for My Past and Future Assassin* (Penguin, 2018), and *To Float in the Space Between: Drawings and Essays in Conversation with Etheridge Knight* (Wave Books, 2018). He was the guest editor of *The Best American Poetry 2014*.

Of "Strange as the Rules of Grammar," Hayes writes: "The title is a mantra. The world is as strange as the rules of grammar."

ROBERT HERSHON (1936–2021) was born in Brooklyn. He received a BA in journalism from New York University. The cofounder and coeditor of Hanging Loose Press and *Hanging Loose* magazine, he was also a celebrated poet. He wrote more than a dozen poetry collections, including *End of the Business Day* (2019), *Calls from the Outside World* (2006), *The German Lunatic* (2000), and *Into a Punchline: Poems 1986–1996* (1994), all from Hanging Loose Press. He was awarded two NEA fellowships and three fellowships from the New York State Foundation for the Arts.

Of "All Right," Caroline Hagood, an editor at *Hanging Loose* writes: "This poem resonates in a world that so often seems to be falling apart around us. Hershon's syntax here mimics the motion of being shunted along in a deluge, trying to hold your head above water. But what his poem also offers that is crucial for us right now, as we bob along in the flood, is his signature Hershonian wit, and warm, playful sense of humor that can deliver up the perfect tragicomic image for the end of the world ('We're burying canned body parts in the garden') and then follow it with lines that are as absurd as they are strangely hopeful—'It's almost / first light, we'll be all right.'"

PAUL HOOVER was born in Harrisonburg, Virginia, in 1946. His most recent book is *O, and Green: New and Selected Poems* (MadHat Press, 2021). With Maria Baranda, he edited and translated *The Complete Poems of San Juan de la Cruz* (Milkweed Editions, 2021). Editor of the annual magazine *New American Writing* and two editions of *Postmodern American Poetry: A Norton Anthology* (1994/2013), he teaches at San Francisco State University.

Of "Admonitions, Afternoons," Hoover writes: "Cole Swensen wrote a very persuasive essay on error's relation to errancy, the model for which is Don Quixote. As writers, we benefit from our errors if we allow ourselves instinctively to stray. I strayed therefore toward the everyday accidents and failures of life, proclaiming their dark charm with the poetic word 'Oh,' which can be spoken in different registers, from dreary to delighted. In the end, of course, we shrug and say, 'It's all good' or 'It will have to do.'"

Born in Manila, Philippines, in 1963, SHELLEY JACKSON is the author of *Riddance* (Catapult, 2018), *Half Life* (HarperCollins, 2006), *The Melancholy of Anatomy* (Anchor, 2002), hypertexts including *Patchwork Girl* (Eastgate, 1995), and several children's books, most recently *Mimi's Dada Catifesto* (Clarion, 2010). Her work has appeared in many journals including *Conjunctions*, *The Paris Review*, *McSweeney's*, and *Cabinet Magazine*. She is also known for her projects SNOW and SKIN: a story published in tattoos on 2,095 volunteers, one word at a time.

Jackson writes: "'Best Original Enigma in Verse' is one of a series of poems I wrote based on page spreads I found on Google Books in which something remains to remind the eye of the physical object left behind when the text was digitized—a turning page, the reader's hand or, in this case, a folded illustration. I discover the poem in the words I find in the image, and this one was inspired by my taste for puzzles as a stealth literary form—the weird language; the way they invite the reader to *do* something with what they read; the way they call out to another, undisclosed text. To my eye, something mortal often seems to haunt them, half-hidden: like the lion in the folded page."

PATRICIA SPEARS JONES, born in Forrest City, Arkansas, in 1951, is a poet, playwright, anthologist, educator, and cultural activist. The winner of the 2017 Jackson Poetry Prize from Poets & Writers, she is author of *A Lucent Fire: New and Selected Poems* (White Pine Press, 2015) and *The Beloved Community* (Copper Canyon Press, 2023). She edited *THINK: Poems for Aretha Franklin's Inauguration Day Hat* and *Ordinary Women: An Anthology of New York City Women Poets*. Mabou Mines commissioned and produced "*Mother*" and *Song For New York: What Women Do When Men Sit Knitting*. She cohosts Open House, a radio program sponsored by Poets House on WBAI.org. She co-curated the Wednesday Night Series for St. Mark's Poetry Project in the 1980s, the first person of color to curate programming there. She has taught at Hollins University, Adelphi University, Hunter College, and Barnard College. She organizes the American Poets Congress and is a Senior Fellow Emeritus of the Black Earth Institute. www.psjones.com.

Of "The Devil's Wife Explains Broken 45s," Jones writes: "I've been writing a series of poems in the voice of the devil's wife—she's not happy. And when Gregory Stephen aka Greg Tate passed away just past his sixty-fourth birthday, it was heartbreaking. Tate was one of those people that you think will live forever, but like those broken 45s, he's gone. The poem is a vehicle for grief and gratitude. It comes out of the joy that Black people make and the virulent resistance to that joy. Like Tate's writing, Brown's dance moves, and my love of poetry—more than traces remain."

ILYA KAMINSKY was born in Odessa, Ukraine, in 1977 and arrived in the United States in 1993, when his family was granted asylum. He is the author of *Dancing in Odessa* (Tupelo Press, 2004) and *Deaf Republic* (Graywolf Press, 2019) as well as coeditor of *The Ecco Anthology of International Poetry* (HarperCollins, 2010) and cotranslator of *Dark Elderberry Branch: Poems of Marina Tsvetaeva* (Alice James Books, 2012). He teaches at Princeton University.

Of "I Ask That I Do Not Die," Kaminsky writes: "This poem is a part of a longer sequence of lyrics, called 'Last Will and Testament.' Why last will and testament? Because at some point we all end up writing one, so I figured I will start mine a tad bit early, and on somewhat lighter terms. Why? Because each lyric poem is the last poem one's going to write. Why? Because lyrics are like little rafts in the wide and stormy sea. You can bite one with your teeth. Or you can stand on top of one and keep paddling while humming a tune."

VINCENT KATZ was born in Manhattan in 1960. He is the author of fourteen books of poetry, including *Broadway for Paul* (Alfred A. Knopf, 2020), *Southness* (Lunar Chandelier Press, 2016), and *Swimming Home* (Nightboat Books, 2015). His translation of *The Complete Elegies of Sextus Propertius* (Princeton University Press, 2004) received the 2005 National Translation Award from the American Literary Translators Association. He is the editor of *Black Mountain College: Experiment in Art* (MIT Press, 2002) and the anthology *Readings in Contemporary Poetry* (Dia Art Foundation, 2017). He lives in New York City.

Of "A Marvelous Sky," Katz writes: "You can almost imagine where this poem was written (I remember it distinctly), but that doesn't really matter. I am often trying to evoke a more generalized sensation of experience and emotion, not one tied to a specific time and place. There's a psalm-like feel to the opening of the poem, transposed into contemporary, quickly changing, times. The presence of 'records' and 'chess shops' puts this in a moment linked to a past that may vanish in the next instant. The narrator is not bothered by that transition, however. Rather, they begin to sense something else in the environment. The *sententia* that begins the second stanza, 'Most people are not excited by their lives,' gets shifted if those people can tune into a feeling of youthfulness that is inexplicably present. Although the air is warm, the season is not specified; it is not spring that causes these feelings, but something more universal and less definable; the air itself carries it. In the final stanza, what is in the air, this possibility of youthfulness accessible to anyone, is associated with music. 'Suddenly' signals the shift in consciousness. The final line is another *sententia*, its decisiveness leavened with the recognition that one may or may not reach those unspecified ones one wants to reach."

Born in 1965 in St. Louis, Missouri, JOHN KEENE is the author, coauthor, and translator of a handful of books including the poetry collection *Punks: New & Selected Poems* (The Song Cave, 2021), which received the 2022 National Book Award for Poetry, the Thom Gunn Award from the Publishing Triangle, and a 2022 Lambda Literary Award for Gay Poetry; and *Counternarratives* (New Directions, 2015), which received an American Book Award, a Lannan Literary Award, and a Windham-Campbell Prize for Fiction. A 2018 MacArthur Fellow, he is a professor at Rutgers University, Newark.

Keene writes: "The title of 'Straight, No Chaser,' derives from a Thelonious Monk song I heard growing up and used to listen to regularly in my twenties during a Monk obsession. The poem itself is anything but 'straight,' though, and through its images, rhythms, and syntax, as well as its New York references, conveys, I hope, a breathless, sometimes staccato, exploration of youthful queer desire, in a mood that is both retrospective & anticipatory of what is to come, the meeting up with the beloved."

MIHO KINNAS was born in Tokyo in 1960. She is the author of two poetry collections, *Today, Fish Only* (2014) and *Move Over, Bird* (2019), both published by Math Paper Press.

Of "Three Shrimp Boats on the Horizon," Kinnas writes: "I clearly remember the day I began this poem. My friends and I were on Hilton Head Island's Coligny beach for the Polar Bear Dip on New Year's Day. I saw three shrimp boats on the horizon as I approached the water. The daytime lacy moon was up, seagulls were flying about, and families flew kites. I was already chanting 'Moon—White Seagulls' as I approached the ocean. Wading into the cold water, I became acutely aware of every element around me. I was so blissful that I became fearful—surely, happiness like this couldn't last. And I began counting my blessings."

WAYNE KOESTENBAUM was born in San Jose, California, in 1958. He has published twenty-two books, including *Ultramarine* (Nightboat, 2022), *The Cheerful Scapegoat: Fables* (Semiotext(e), 2021), *Figure It Out: Essays* (Soft Skull, 2020), *The Pink Trance Notebooks* (Nightboat, 2015), *My 1980s & Other Essays* (Farrar, Straus and Giroux, 2013), and *The Queen's Throat* (Poseidon, 1993). In 2020 he received an American Academy of Arts and Letters Award in Literature. Yale's Beinecke Rare Book and Manuscript Library acquired his literary archive in 2019. He is a Distinguished Professor of English, French, and Comparative Literature at CUNY Graduate Center.

Koestenbaum writes: " '[Misread "master craftsman"]' is number thirty-two in a series of thirty-six quasi-sonnets, a book manuscript I now call *Stubble Archipelago*. Many of these poems I wrote while walking around New York City. I'd jot down phrases in my notebook or dictate them into my phone. At home, I'd incorporate these fragmented gleanings into whatever sonnet I happened to be composing that day. Therefore each poem functions as a coded diary entry, including specific references to sidewalk events and peripatetic perceptions, squeezed into the stringent but elastic format of the fourteen lines, each line permitted to spawn several indented tributary lines, as in an old-fashioned 'bob-and-wheel' poem."

YUSEF KOMUNYAKAA was born in Bogalusa, Louisiana, in 1947. He served in Vietnam. His most recent collection, *Everyday Mojo Songs of Earth: New and Selected Poems*, was published by Farrar, Straus and

Giroux in 2021. He recently retired from teaching in the creative writing program at New York University. He was the guest editor of *The Best American Poetry 2003*.

Komunyakaa writes: "This excerpt from *Autobiography of My Alter Ego* delves into the war in Vietnam with a glancing blow of satire. The narrator of the poem is a White veteran. Here, he's a prisoner of war in a dream, touching on the moment when Senator John McCain was lambasted by a laughable joker from central casting who seems to have gotten away with public ridicule of an American POW. McCain possessed clout because of his military service, but also his lineage is heroic and honorable. Vets I've talked to, for the most part, see this put-down artist as merely a coward. In fact, it is next to impossible not to view McCain's inquisitor as a malingerer talking packaged malarkey. Indeed, the mention of heel spurs is more than a laugh. Plus, it's hard to say the name of this character who relies on inherited hierarchy—even if it has nothing to do with goldmine lore. I wrote these lines also to hear Alan Benditt (an actor friend who has memorized the thirty-odd sections of the poem) speak the lines—not even saying this anti-hero's name—who probably would have been fragged in Nam if he hadn't escaped with his damn heel spurs."

MICHAEL LALLY was born in 1942 in Orange, New Jersey, into a large Irish American family and clan including cops, priests, musicians, and political activists. He started out as a jazz musician in the late 1950s and was an enlisted man in the U.S. Air Force from 1962 to 1966, after which he attended the University of Iowa on the GI Bill. A Civil Rights and antiwar activist, he ran for Sheriff of Johnson County, Iowa, on the Peace and Freedom Party ticket in 1968. He has been an activist for women's and gay rights from 1969 to the present. His thirtieth and latest book is *Another Way to Play: Poems 1960–2017* (Seven Stories Press, 2018). From 1966 to 1984 he reviewed books for such publications as *The Washington Post* and the *Village Voice*. From 1979 to 2009 he worked as a scriptwriter and actor on television shows and films including *NYPD Blue*, *Deadwood*, and *White Fang*.

Of "I Meant To," Lally writes: "When I sent out emails to invite friends to my eightieth birthday party, my arthritic Parkinson's shaky hand hit cc instead of bcc and it brought up all the ways in which things I meant to do turn out differently in my old age. From the phrase 'I meant to,' a natural rhythm emerged to support a litany of actual 'I meant to' moments that had recently occurred. I'm grateful that my learned response to disappointment is to turn it into poetry."

DOROTHEA LASKY was born in St. Louis, Missouri, in 1978. She is the author of seven books of poetry and prose, including *Animal* (Wave Books, 2019).

Lasky writes: "My poem 'Green Moon' is indebted to 'Romance Sonámbulo' by Federico García Lorca, 'From the Desire Field' by Natalie Diaz, and 'Talk' by Noelle Kocot. I've long been fascinated by the power of the color green, how odd and elegant it is, and how it symbolizes love and desire in the most unexpected ways. It's the opposite of red on the color wheel and perhaps it is haunted by the memory of red and all its associated passions. Green also somehow contains the mood of regret. Of course, I would want my poem to mean so many things to its readers, but for me it's about the romantic possibility of regret."

DAVID LEHMAN is the series editor of *The Best American Poetry*.

Of "Traces," Lehman writes: "By August 1, 2020, the Covid pandemic had settled in, and no end seemed in sight. Locked down, I decided to renew an old habit and write a poem every day. On the eighth of the month, the date itself provided the stimulus I needed to recover memories of my life in New York City the summer before my sophomore year of college. When *The Paris Review* printed the original 'Traces' in its Spring 1968 issue, the date of composition (8/8/67) was included. It was my first appearance in *The Paris Review*."

ADA LIMÓN is the author of six books of poetry including, most recently, *The Hurting Kind* (Milkweed Editions, 2022). In 2022, she was named the twenty-fourth Poet Laureate of the United States.

Limón writes: "In many ways, 'Hooky' is a poem for wonder. I wrote it thinking of those days when, out of nowhere, the world would open up, would allow for tenderness, would reveal some sort of secret beauty underneath its restrictions and chaos. I have always been someone who wanted approval and good grades and yet some of my most meaningful experiences have come out of wandering, out of getting lost, out of allowing myself to stare at trees for a very long time and do nothing but watch how they moved in the wind."

J. Estanislao Lopez is the author of *We Borrowed Gentleness* (Alice James Books, 2022). He lives and teaches in his hometown, Houston.

Of "Places with Terrible Wi-Fi," Lopez writes: "This poem began with the title, taken from an overheard complaint. Once I found a first line that created a kind of forward thrust, I let music and association do their work. The title creates an imperative to write in the mode of a catalog, but I think what makes the poem most successful is its ability to subvert that rhetorical pattern at certain moments, giving the poem just enough instability to feel alive."

Kimberly Lyons was born in Tucson, Arizona, and grew up in Chicago. Lyons was a teen participant in the Urban Gateways workshops. She studied at Columbia College and graduated from Bard College in 1981. She was a program coordinator at the Poetry Project for five years and has hosted events at Anthology Film Archives, the Zinc Bar, bookstores, and conferences nationally. Among Lyons's books of poetry are a limited edition with Granary Books *Mettle* (1996), *Calcinatio* (Faux Press, 2014), *Approximately Near* (Metambesendotorg, 2016), and *Capella* (Oread Press, 2018). She lives in Brooklyn, New York.

Of "Coffee with Lavender," Lyons writes: "I used to write poems in cafés quite often. But not for years. One morning, I pulled out my notebook while enjoying a coffee in a local café in Brooklyn. Perhaps the sheer gratitude to be outside in the light, among people, in 2021, led to a poem that unfolded from reception of taste to a complex of language that surprised me with its dark intensity and latitude. This is the strange intentionality of poetry."

Bernadette Mayer (1945–2022) was born in Brooklyn and lived most of her life in New York City. She is one of the most iconic and innovative poets associated with the New York School, an important influence on scores of writers who took her legendary workshops at The New School, St. Mark's Poetry Project, and privately. Her many books include *Midwinter Day* (Turtle Island, 1982; New Directions,

1999), *A Bernadette Mayer Reader* (New Directions, 1992), *The Desires of Mothers to Please Others in Letters* (New Directions, 1994), *Works and Days* (New Directions, 2016), and *Milkweed Smithereens* (New Directions, 2022). In 2015 she received a Guggenheim Fellowship.

Of "Pi-Day," guest editor Elaine Equi writes: "Mayer offers a dazzling example of the genre of the occasional poem. Pi-Day is March 14, a holiday invented by physicist Larry Shaw, chosen because 3/14 represents the first three digits of this mathematical sign. It is also Albert Einstein's birthday. Mayer's poem is a jazzy improvisation on these facts, punning on Pi and pie—and in the process offering startling reflections such as, 'I am within / the realm / of figuring out / how everybody twinkles / on this day / like clouds / through icicles.' She is the perfect poet to capture the magical intersection of mathematics and the mundane."

Born in Syracuse, New York, in 1967, MAUREEN N. MCLANE is the author of eight books of poetry, including *Some Say* (Farrar, Straus and Giroux, 2017) and *This Blue* (FSG, 2014), as well as a hybrid of memoir and criticism, *My Poets* (FSG, 2012). She has written two critical monographs on British romantic poetics and numerous essays on romantic and contemporary literature and culture. Her poems have been translated into French, Greek, Spanish, Italian, and Czech. Her most recent book is *What You Want* (FSG and Penguin UK, 2023). She teaches poetry and poetics at New York University. She likes anthologies, alphabets, & ampersands.

McLane writes: " 'Moonrise' was drafted in April 2021, in upstate New York, a year or so into the pandemic. It condenses many things—a moonrise (or many); moons in poems like Coleridge's 'Dejection Ode' and old ballads like 'Sir Patrick Spens'; restorative conversations and pandemic pulses toward connection; provisional optimism amid ambient dread; thoughts beamed from and across Lake Champlain over the Atlantic toward Europe, and westward toward the Pacific, and wherever friends and comrades might yet be. As Lisa Robertson has written, 'this is for friendship.' "

DUNYA MIKHAIL was born in Iraq in 1965 and came to the United States in 1996. Her books include *The Bird Tattoo* (Pegasus Books,

2022), *In Her Feminine Sign* (New Directions, 2019), and *The Beekeeper: Rescuing the Stolen Women of Iraq* (New Directions, 2018). *The Iraqi Nights* (New Directions, 2014) received the Poetry Magazine Translation Award, *Diary of a Wave Outside the Sea* (New Directions, 2009) won the Arab American Book Award, and *The War Works Hard* (New Directions, 2005) was shortlisted for the Griffin Poetry Prize. She lectures on Arabic and poetry at Oakland University in Michigan.

Mikhail writes: " 'Tablets' is named after Sumerian repositories of the world's first writing. I wrote them in Arabic first then in English. Another layer of translation I practiced in these tablets is transferring them from words to images. I mean I drew them primitively, in harmony with the spirit of those simple signs in their first communication with the world."

STEPHEN PAUL MILLER's poetry previously appeared in *The Best American Poetry 1994*. Born on Staten Island, New York, in 1951, he is the author of twelve books of poetry and cultural studies, such as *Art Is Boring for the Same Reason We Stayed in Vietnam* (Domestic Press and Unmuzzled Ox, 1992), *The Seventies Now: Culture as Surveillance* (Duke University Press, 1999), *The Bee Flies in May* (Marsh Hawk Press, 2003), *Being with a Bullet* (Talisman House Publishers, 2007), *Fort Dad* (Marsh Hawk, 2009), *There's Only One God and You're Not It* (Marsh Hawk, 2011), *Any Lie You Tell Will Be the Truth* (Marsh Hawk, 2015), *The New Deal as a Triumph of Social Work: Frances Perkins and the Confluence of Early Twentieth Century Social Work and Mid-Twentieth Century Politics and Government* (Palgrave Macmillan, 2015), and the forthcoming *Dating Buddha* (Marsh Hawk Press). With Terence Diggory, Miller coedited *The Scene of My Selves: New Work on New York School Poetry* (National Poetry Foundation, 2001); he is also a coeditor of *Radical Poetics and Secular Jewish Culture* (University of Alabama Press, 2009). Having completed his PhD in American Studies at New York University in 1990, Miller was a Senior Fulbright Scholar at Jagiellonian University in Krakow, Poland (1996–1997). He is a professor of English at St. John's University in New York.

Miller writes: "A chance hearing of The Who's song 'Getting in Tune' helped induce me to write 'Dating Buddha.' Peter Townshend said the song is one of many he wrote as 'a devout and committed devotee of Meher Baba, an Indian spiritual master,' and I noted that Townshend likened the master–aspirant relationship to a romantic one with lines such as 'Do you come here often?' This led to the thought of 'dating Buddha.' Perhaps more importantly, the song is reflexive in the sense that, as it describes 'getting in tune' with a spiritual master, it literally establishes its melodic 'tune.' Its lyrics move from an encounter with a 'note' sung merely because 'it fits in well with the chords I'm playing,' to a singer's admission that he 'can't pretend there's any meaning hidden in the things I'm saying,' and finally to a focused effort to 'tune / right in on you.' Similarly, 'Dating Buddha' establishes a poetic groove as it ponders what it might be like to date Buddha. To develop this groove, I wrote a long list of many pages detailing the 'heaven' in my everyday world and my imagination. The notion that getting in tune with Buddha would involve losing the illusion of a fixed perspective informed this list. It occurred to me that dating Buddha would necessarily be one oddly wonderful disillusionment after another. I was influenced by Meher Baba saying that Buddha made one 'divine mistake' so as not to destroy the illusion of creation with his manifestation of complete truth. Buddha, according to Baba, intentionally overemphasized the 'I am nothing' state over its paradoxically complementary state of 'I am everything.' I thus tried to balance a lovely nothingness with endless possibility. After many months of adding to my list, I realized that the poem required scrupulous editing to establish the poetic groove that seemed essential to 'Dating Buddha.' Over several more months, I condensed and deleted from my list. Then I forgot all about the poem. I want to thank Daniel Morris for making me think more about it by selecting it for the *Marsh Hawk Review* and Elaine Equi and David Lehman for including it here."

Poet, essayist, and translator SUSAN MITCHELL was born and raised in Brooklyn, New York. She has written three books of poems and been honored with fellowships from the Guggenheim Foundation, the Lannan Foundation, and the National Endowment for the Arts. Her collection *Rapture* (HarperCollins, 1992) won the Kingsley Tufts Poetry Award, and was one of five National Book Award finalists. She is the Mary Blossom Lee Professor in Poetry at Florida Atlantic University.

Mitchell writes: "How I came to write 'Chopin in Palma' was very different from how I usually write poems. I had given a reading of new work and, to explain what I was doing in some of my poems, had commented on two of Chopin's twenty-four Preludes. After the reading, a concert pianist, very interested in my observations about Chopin's compositions, came up to talk to me. By that time I had forgotten most of what I had said extemporaneously that this pianist found remarkable. So, I must have been creating as I talked and been in the altered or waking dream state that for me accompanies writing. Fortunately, I had recorded my reading, and as I listened later to my comments—and I have to confess most of the playback was news to me—I began jotting down lines and phrases that had to do with music, tempo, desire, and crossing boundaries. 'Chopin in Palma' grew out of these jottings, as did other related poems, most of them now published or 'waiting to hear.' Of course, this does not explain who exactly speaks 'Chopin in Palma.' A cosmopolitan narrator—yes. A narrator that is a composite of—? The term I have invented for my speaker is the 'polyphonic narrator'—a narrator who speaks from both inside and outside his own temporal boundaries. How did this narrator come into being? Perhaps mysteries should be left to associate with each other, copulating and reproducing as the ancients believed minerals did—underground in the dark."

VALZHYNA MORT is the author of three poetry collections, most recently, *Music for the Dead and Resurrected: Poems* (Farrar, Straus and Giroux, 2020), which won the International Griffin Poetry Prize and the UNT Rilke Prize. Her two previous collections are *Factory of Tears* and *Collected Body* (both Copper Canyon Press, 2008 and 2011). She has been honored with fellowships from the Guggenheim Foundation, the American Academy in Rome, the Lannan Foundation, and the Amy Clampitt Foundation. She has received a National Endowment for the Arts grant for her translation work. Born in Minsk, Belarus, Mort writes in English and Belarusian. She lives in Ithaca, New York.

Mort writes: " 'Extraordinary Life of Tadeusz Kościuszko in Several Invoices' tells a story of famous freedom fighter Tadeusz Kościuszko, who rose against the dividing powers of the two empires, Prussia and Russia. Kościuszko led the Polish uprising of 1794, was captured, and jailed by Catherine II. For Poland, he is a national hero, and in the United States bridges and streets are named after him; a military engineer, he fought on the American side in the American War of Independence. In my poem, however, I'm interested in a more private Kościuszko: a lonely, 'homeless' man from a cabbage farm in what is today Belarus, a self-made man with an unpronounceable name, whose ghost, after a life of depression and unreturned love, still cannot rest. A fervent abolitionist, he engaged in a lifelong correspondence with Thomas Jefferson, a relationship often described as 'friendship,' yet, it was anything but. When Kościuszko left the United States, he made Jefferson his financial executor and requested that money be used for the manumission of the enslaved people at Monticello. When Jefferson refused, their correspondence grew more and more passive-aggressive and bitter. The bitter ironies of history are such that after the defeat of Kościuszko's uprising by the Russian Empire, Russian generals, just like American ones, were paid in humans: thousands of Belarusian peasants were 'gifted' to Russians as bounty. Kościuszko's ethical, worldly life appears utopian, and, at once, despite his posthumous glory, so utterly sad and restless. His final wish was never fulfilled."

HARRYETTE MULLEN, born in Alabama in 1953, grew up in Texas and lives in California. Her poetry collections include *Sleeping with the Dictionary* (University of California Press, 2002), *Recyclopedia: Trimmings, S*PeRM**K*T, and Muse & Drudge* (Graywolf Press, 2006), and *Urban Tumbleweed: Notes from a Tanka Diary* (Graywolf, 2013). Black Sunflowers Press will publish *Open Leaves / poems from earth* in 2023. Her *Silver-Tongued Companion*, a critical edition of collected and uncollected poems, is forthcoming from Edinburgh University Press.

Of "As I Wander Lonely in the Cloud," Mullen writes: "As with Shakespeare's 'Sonnet 130' that inspired my own 'Dim Lady' and 'Variation on a Theme Park' in *Sleeping with the Dictionary*, I enjoy occasional collaborations with the canon of English poetry, in this case rewriting an iconic lyric of British Romanticism. I'm certainly not the first or last to riff on one of Wordsworth's greatest hits."

KATHLEEN OSSIP was born in Albany, New York. Her books of poems include *July* (Sarabande, 2021); *The Do-Over* (Sarabande, 2015); *The*

Cold War (Sarabande, 2011); and *The Search Engine* (APR/Copper Canyon Press, 2002), which Derek Walcott selected for the American Poetry Review/Honickman First Book Prize. "The Facts" appears in *Little Poems* (Verve Poetry Press, 2022). She has received a fellowship from the New York Foundation for the Arts, and has been a fellow at the Radcliffe Institute, Harvard University. She teaches at the New School and at Princeton University.

Ossip writes: "I'm usually a wait and hurry up kind of writer, with more waiting than hurrying up, but during the early months of the pandemic I found that poems came quickly and easily. A big part of my social life during that time was swapping poems with a friend, then Zooming to talk about them. 'The Facts' was one of these poems. I wrote it pretty automatically and didn't question it much. I may have fiddled around with the form and the breaks, and I think the part about the meadow was added in a second go-round. I didn't consciously intend social commentary, but since I wrote it during the long chaos of misinformation following January 2020, it's clear now what my unconscious was up to."

EUGENE OSTASHEVSKY was born in 1968 in the city that was then known as Leningrad in the USSR. He grew up in New York and now lives mainly in Berlin. *The Feeling Sonnets*, published in 2022 by Carcanet in the UK and NYRB Poets in the United States, examines the effects of speaking a nonnative language on emotions, parenting, and identity. An earlier book, *The Pirate Who Does Not Know the Value of Pi* (NYRB Poets, 2017), discusses communication difficulties between pirates and parrots. Its German translation by Uljana Wolf and Monika Rink won the City of Münster International Poetry Prize. His other books of poetry, *The Life and Opinions of DJ Spinoza* and *Iterature*, were published by Ugly Duckling Presse in 2008 and 2005. As a translator, Ostashevsky is best known for his *OBERIU: An Anthology of Russian Absurdism* (Northwestern University Press, 2006) and Alexander Vvedensky's *An Invitation for Me to Think* (with Matvei Yankelevich; NYRB Poets, 2013), which won the National Translation Award.

Of "from *The Feeling Sonnets*," Ostashevsky writes: "My poetry stresses the fact that English is not entirely my native language. It is translingual, in that I think about differences in the ways languages divide and interpret the world, and also in that I cannot speak about things without speaking about speaking about things. Like much trans-lingual poetry, mine is the poetry of wordplay and linguistic estrangement. Puns let it consider words and expressions from the outside, as things rather than signs. Multiplicity of puns renders language ambivalent and polyphonic, as the meanings of the same words parallel, transform into, or contradict one another. Puns are often disparaged in English but not by me. I construct the poem from the sound and look of words, trying to bring together ones that are as formally similar as possible and as semantically different as possible. The system of formal similarities between words is unique to each language. For example, I know of no other language where 'heard' incorporates an anagram of 'read': where this particular formal relation arises between those two meanings. This is how my poetry expresses the fact that we make meaning from chance."

Born in 1950, YUKO OTOMO is a visual artist and a bilingual (Japa-nese/English) writer of Japanese origin. She writes poetry, haiku, art criticism, travelogues, and essays. Her publications include *Garden: Selected Haiku* (Beehive Press, 2000); *STUDY & Other Poems on Art* (Ugly Duckling Presse, 2013); *FROZEN HEATWAVE*, a collabora-tive linked poem project with Steve Dalachinsky (Luna Bisonte Prods, 2017); *Anonymous Landscape* (Lithic Press, 2019); *In Delacroix's Gar-den*, a collaborative book with Basil King (Spuyten Duyvil, 2022); and *PINK* (Lithic Press, 2023). She lives in New York City.

Of "Sunday Cave," Otomo writes: "The more I love my own spe-cies, the more misanthropic & remote I become. One Sunday after-noon, the interior darkness of the downtown NYC old tenement apartment where I live & the music became the portal to carry me to the essential depth of the meaning of being here now."

Born in Graceville, Minnesota, in 1943, MAUREEN OWEN is the for-mer editor-in-chief of *Telephone Magazine* and Telephone Books. She coordinated the St. Mark's Poetry Project. Her books include *Ero-sion's Pull* (Coffee House Press, 2006) and *American Rush: Selected Poems* (Talisman House, 1998). *AE (Amelia Earhart)* (Vortex Editions, 1984) received the Before Columbus American Book Award. She has taught at Naropa University and edited Naropa's online zine *not enough night* through nineteen issues. Her recent books are *Edges of Water* (Chax Press, 2013) *let the heart hold down the breakage   Or   the caregiver's log* (Hanging Loose Press, 2022). A recipient of grants from the National Endowment for the Arts and the Foundation for Contemporary Arts, she can be found reading her work on the PennSound website.

Of "In space   surface tension will force / a small blob of liquid   to form a sphere," Owen writes: "Caring for my mom was, as it is for all of those needing care, a twenty-four seven commitment. Mornings and twilights and midnights and dawn, all blended into one fabric, one long, flowing skein of water that swirled and swept ever forward. Too tired to journal or record, I managed a few wild sentences some nights, scribbled down in haste in a rumpled notebook I pulled off a kitchen shelf. I never intended them to become a work. Rather it seemed a way to hold on to some clarity, some sanity, and to hold on to my mother in those fleeting, heartrending times.

"It was some time after her passing that I felt able to pull the notebook down one morning. It was a jumble of scrawls, but reality in its barest truth. The realness of caring for someone you hold so close, love so much, and yet here was the darkness of that closure in all its honesty."

XAN PHILLIPS, a poet and visual artist from rural Ohio, has received a Whiting Award, a Lambda Literary Award, and the Judith A. Markowitz Award for emerging writers. Xan is the author of *HULL* (Nightboat Books, 2019) and *Reasons for Smoking*, which won the 2016 Seattle Review Chapbook contest judged by Claudia Rankine. He has received fellowships from Brown University, Callaloo, Cave Canem, The Conversation Literary Festival, the Wisconsin Institute for Creative Writing, the Sewanee Writers Conference, and the Center for African American Poetry and Poetics.

KATHA POLLITT was born in 1949 and grew up in New York City, where she still lives. She writes a regular column in *The Nation*, focusing on politics, feminism, and the occasional book or movie. Her most recent book of poems is *The Mind-Body Problem* (Random House, 2009; Seren Books, 2012). Her most recent book of prose is *Pro:*

Reclaiming Abortion Rights (Picador, 2014). She lives on the Upper West Side with her husband, Steven Lukes, and their cat, Patsy, and is (she writes) "still trying to learn German!"

Pollitt writes: "I wrote 'Brown Furniture' in hopes of dissuading my longtime friend from remodeling her friendly old kitchen into something cold and contemporary. It worked! I love old things—old furniture, old china, old books, old writers, old music, and of course my friends. My dream is to have a used-book store and just sit there reading and writing and chatting with people who drop by, as long as there aren't very many of them."

CAROLYN MARIE RODGERS (1940–2010) was born in Chicago and grew up on the city's South Side. She received her MA in English from the University of Chicago. Rodgers was an important figure in the Black Arts Movement in the 1960s. Her many books include *Paper Soul* (Third World, 1968); *Songs of a Black Bird* (Third World, 1969), which won the Poet Laureate Award of the Society of Midland Authors; and *how i got ovah: new and selected poems* (Anchor Press, 1975).

Of "Poem No. 2: My Kind of Feminism," guest editor Elaine Equi writes: "I'm happy to include this poem by a woman writer from Chicago, the city I'm originally from. I was attracted by the way Rodgers uses a surprising extended car metaphor to talk about integrating the different sides of her being, from the biological, to the psychological, to the social, to the spiritual: 'Parts of the spirit, / introverted body members, / aspects in the soul.' In the space of this short poem, she shows us the transformation from the mechanical, compartmentalized model of the car, to the exquisite organic image at the end: 'My living, exfoliating, / like a black multifoliate rose.'"

JEROME SALA was born in Evergreen Park, Illinois, in 1951. He is the author of eight collections of poetry, the latest of which is *How Much? New and Selected Poems* (NYQ Books, 2022). He worked for more than thirty years writing ads, TV commercials, and promotional materials for major advertising agencies and magazines. Now he devotes his time to poetry and essay writing. He has a PhD in American Studies from New York University. He lives in New York City.

Of "Something I've Not Bought" Sala writes: "I love the satiric tradition of poetry. One of the methods I use to satirize aspects of our everyday life is to translate metaphysical poems into contemporary, secular language. My poem is a nearly line-by-line rewrite of W. S. Merwin's 'Something I've Not Done.' In Merwin's poem, the poet is haunted by an uncompleted task his destiny demands. In my version, the poet is haunted by the internet's tracking technology. He has looked at a product on a website but not made a purchase. Now, everywhere in his digital life, he encounters ads for this item urging him to fulfill his duty as a consumer."

Born in 1976 in San Antonio, Texas, JASON SCHNEIDERMAN is the author of four books of poems: *Hold Me Tight* (Red Hen Press, 2020), *Primary Source* (Red Hen, 2016), *Striking Surface* (Ashland Poetry Press, 2010), and *Sublimation Point* (Four Way Books, 2004). He edited the anthology *Queer: A Reader for Writers* (Oxford University Press, 2016). A professor of English at the Borough of Manhattan Community College, he teaches in the MFA Program for Writers at Warren Wilson College and is one of the curators of the Monday night poetry reading series at KGB Bar in New York City. "Dramaturgy" will appear in his forthcoming collection, *Self-Portrait of Icarus as a Country on Fire*, from Red Hen in 2024.

Schneiderman writes: "Thank you to everyone who asked to see the play described in 'Dramaturgy' or otherwise suggested that they thought that the poem was based in autobiographical fact. The poem is entirely made up, though every time I say this, I find myself explaining that many of the details are true. The horribly, cheerfully, athletically Auschwitz-themed ice-dancing routine on the Russian reality show really did happen in November 2016. You can find it on YouTube. My mother did tell me that her mother, upon learning what had happened to her European relatives, burned the photo albums that contained their images. It is true that in 2016, shortly after Donald Trump's election, I took a shirt out of my closet and when I looked in the mirror to check the fit, I discovered that I was still in only an undershirt and that I had folded the shirt as if to pack it.

"I grew up in a time of great optimism. I had a sense of history as an arc that bent toward justice, that led from a backward past to a forward present. Events from history felt distant (historical!), and events in the present felt current, but now I have the sense that time and place have collapsed. In Florida, Anita Bryant's late 1970s *Save Our Children* campaign has been revived as *Don't Say Gay*. In Michigan, a 1931 law against abortion came back onto the books. The spirit of Anthony Comstock seemed to have returned in the shape of a censorious gubernatorial campaign in Virginia. Someone stormed the Capitol wearing a Camp Auschwitz sweatshirt. Someone storming the Capitol shat in the hallway. When I read *The New York Times*, I feel like I've slipped into a *Doctor Who* season finale in which all the villains from all the times have converged into a single battle against decency and goodness. Except it's not exciting, and the outcome is far from guaranteed.

"One definition of trauma is an event from the past that will not stay in the past. The traumatic event is not remembered but relived. For many groups there are traumas that are central to their collective identities, and they retell those traumas not merely to reinforce their group identities but because there are outside forces who insist that their traumas are not traumas at all. Because I am a Jew, I know the curious logic of that denial: the only people who deny the holocaust are the ones who think it was a good idea. Holocaust deniers wish the 'final solution' had been completed, while insisting it was never carried out at all. I cannot fully parse what it meant to me to see those ice dancers dressed in the striped pajamas and yellow stars of Auschwitz. Was it a trivialization of the holocaust? A denial? A mockery? A celebration? I still don't know. But I know it made me feel like I had to change something or leave somewhere, and that was the genesis of the poem."

TIM SEIBLES was born in Philadelphia in 1955. He is the author of several poetry collections including *Hurdy-Gurdy* (Cleveland State University Poetry Center, 1992); *Buffalo Head Solos* (Cleveland State University Poetry Center, 2004); and *Fast Animal* (Etruscan Press, 2012), which won the Theodore Roethke Memorial Poetry Prize. Tim completed a two-year appointment as poet laureate of Virginia (2016–18). *Voodoo Libretto*, a collection of his new and selected poems, was released by Etruscan in 2022.

Of "All the Time Blues Villanelle," Seibles writes: "After losing someone, we usually cannot help recalling those phrases s/he offered as *wisdom to live by*. One of the repeating lines in this villanelle features something my father often said which, for mysterious reasons, regularly recurs to me. Because a villanelle is built on repetition, this form seemed a perfect container for both my grief about the loss and my delight in his voice."

DIANE SEUSS is the author five books of poems, including *frank: sonnets* (Graywolf Press, 2021), winner of the PEN/Voelcker Prize, the Los Angeles Times Book Prize, the National Book Critics Circle Award, and the Pulitzer Prize. Among her previous books are *Still Life with Two Dead Peacocks and a Girl* (Graywolf, 2018) and *Four-Legged Girl* (Graywolf, 2015). Her sixth collection, *Modern Poetry*, is forthcoming from Graywolf in 2024. A 2020 Guggenheim Fellow, she received the John Updike Award from the American Academy of Arts and Letters in 2021. She was born in Michigan City, Indiana, in 1956, and was raised by a single mother in rural Michigan, which she continues to call home.

Seuss writes: "'Little Fugue (State)' is the opening poem of my forthcoming collection, *Modern Poetry*, in which musical genres and compositional types are one of the book's motifs. (I can't say I know much about music; I've had to learn.) This poem does not attempt to replicate a classical fugue, but is simply suggestive of the fugue's use of echo and circulation, almost as if it chases its subject. I was also interested in the psychological definition of 'fugue,' a period of lostness, amnesia, sometimes in response to a traumatic event. It is a state in which I have often found myself, especially since the onset of the coronavirus pandemic and the preceding and ensuing social and political chaos. The poem does not mention those subjects. It is set in the landscape of my upbringing, and in an interior landscape, therefore its image palette is primal—hair, brush, underbrush, body, bee, breath. This speaker does not know where she is. Can't acclimate herself. The end of the poem introduces the poem's and book's true subject—that the speaker, *I*, cannot remember what poetry is, what it can accomplish, where this, my life's work, 'this dog I've walked and walked / to death,' is heading, and what it can possibly mean. It is a small overture to a crisis of the spirit."

DAVID SHAPIRO was a violin prodigy in an artistic family in his youth. His eleven books of poetry include *January* (Holt, Rinehart and Winston, 1965), published when he was an eighteen-year-old undergraduate; *New and Selected Poems, 1965–2006* (Overlook Press, 2013); and *In Memory of an Angel* (City Lights, 2017). After earning a BA/MA from Clare College, Cambridge University, as a Kellett Fellow, then a PhD from Columbia University, Shapiro taught at Columbia, William Patterson University, and The Cooper Union, while producing numerous prose works, including monographs on John Ashbery, Jasper Johns, and Piet Mondrian. Shapiro's *You Are the You: Writings and Interviews on Poetry, Art, and the New York School*—introduced by David Lehman and edited by Kate Farrell—is forthcoming from MadHat Press in spring 2024.

On August 2, 1962, John Ashbery wrote a long, detailed letter to David Shapiro that begins: "I find your poems very beautiful. In fact, I can think of few poets writing today whose work gives me so much pleasure and excitement. This would be amazing for a poet of any age, and I simply can't 'digest' the fact that you're only fifteen."

Shapiro writes: "'A Lost Poem of Jesus' is really a fiction about the difficulty of understanding the earliest days of the primitive Church. The pathos of this poem is a bit wild and a bit open. I'm aware in my poetry of the very idea of a fiction that need never end."

MITCH SISSKIND grew up in Chicago, attended Columbia University, and now lives in Los Angeles. Recent books of poetry include *Collected Poems 2005–2020* (Burrow Books, 2020) and *Do Not Be a Gentleman When You Say Goodnight* (The Song Cave, 2016). His two books of short fiction are *Visitations* (Brightwaters Press, 1984) and *Dog Man Stories* (Wise Acre, 1993). Sisskind's poems were included in *The Best American Poetry* in 2009 and 2013.

Of "Only Death Wows Me," Sisskind writes: "According to Jewish tradition, reciting the sacred 'sh'ma' prayer with your last breath brings immediate entrance to heaven. (Keep that in mind!) However, when Steve Jobs faced eternity he said 'WOW.' For me that calls to mind a passage in Walter Isaacson's biography: Jobs 'was not especially intelligent, but he was a genius.' Yes, it was an act of genius to link those two great words, WOW and death. I was inspired to write a poem about it. In the same poem there's something about finding the 'dead person's false teeth lying around.' That's based on a true story. But to spare my survivors such a challenging moment, I'm going to take my false teeth with me. I'll have the best teeth in the cemetery."

Writer, musician, and marketing professional, JACK SKELLEY was born in the Los Angeles suburb of Torrance, California, in 1956. His books include *Monsters* (Little Caesar Press, 1982), *Dennis Wilson and Charlie Manson* (Fred & Barney Press, 2021), *Interstellar Theme Park: New and Selected Writing* (BlazeVOX [books], 2022), and *The Complete Fear of Kathy Acker* (Semiotext(e), 2023). Skelley is guitarist and songwriter for the psychedelic surf band Lawndale (SST Records).

Of "Green Goddess," Skelley writes: "Ingredients include: raunchy appetite, apotheosis, Edenic nostalgia, hawt lingerie, consumer reports, monotheism dethroned, and worshipful pussy-eating (may I say that?). No oil necessary."

AMANDA SMELTZ is the author of *Imperial Bender*, her debut poetry collection. She was honored with a 2021 writing fellowship with The Mastheads in Pittsfield, Massachusetts. She lives in Jersey City and works in wine import and distribution in New York City.

Of "These Squatting Girls in Black Spandex," Smeltz writes: "This poem arose out of my being in a yoga class and looking around the room and seeing every student—almost entirely cisgendered white women—squatting in matching black athletic leggings. I remember thinking: surely this can't be what the yoga sutras were talking about. Then I thought about all the other times I've thought: surely this can't be what they were talking about when they talked about *x*, in all manner of spiritual, religious, and meditative arenas. And yet, repeatedly I find myself in such spaces anyway. We're always looking for that slippery something *more*; it's hard to know where to find it."

Born in the San Francisco Bay Area in 1955, COLE SWENSEN is the author of nineteen volumes of poetry, the most recent of which are *And And And* (Free Poetry, Boise State University, 2022) and *Art in Time* (Nightboat Books, 2021). She also has a volume of critical essays, *Noise That Stays Noise* (from the University of Michigan's Poets on Poetry Series, 2011). She coedited the Norton anthology *American*

Hybrid (2009). Previously on the faculties of the University of Denver and the Iowa Writers' Workshop, she currently teaches at Brown University and divides her time between the United States and France, where she translates French poetry and art criticism.

Of "Various Gloves," Swensen writes: "I've recently been fascinated by the question of *what a thing is*—largely because, of course, a thing never ends; it can never be separated from its interactions and collaborations with everything around it. So, asking the question when focused on a specific thing has offered a way to open up the thing in question and explore the various networks that it's involved in. The series focuses on both animals and objects—often intricately entangled."

ARTHUR SZE was born in New York City in 1950. His eleven books of poetry include *The Glass Constellation: New and Collected Poems* (Copper Canyon Press, 2021) and *Sight Lines*, which won the 2019 National Book Award for Poetry. He received a 2022 Ruth Lilly Poetry Prize for lifetime achievement from the Poetry Foundation as well as the Shelley Memorial Award from the Poetry Society of America. He is a professor emeritus at the Institute of American Indian Arts.

Sze writes: "On April 6, 2022, the U.S. Forest Service started a prescribed burn, but unexpected winds blew the flames across containment lines. The Calf Canyon/Hermit's Peak Fire burned 341,735 acres and became the largest wildfire in New Mexico history. As I wrote 'Wildfire Season,' I started with wind, smoke, and images from the fire, but other pressures enlarged and deepened the poem. As interconnection, and on a planetary scale, the image of an Inuit singer who stretches walrus bladder and completes a box drum came to mind. And as I wrote, I recognized that the poem was moving ahead of what I could understand, so I just trusted that motion."

DIANE THIEL was born in Coral Gables, Florida, in 1967 and grew up in Miami Beach. She is the author of eleven books of poetry and nonfiction. Her latest book of poetry, *Questions from Outer Space*, appeared in 2022 from Red Hen Press. Her other books include *EchoLocations* (Story Line Press, 2000), which received the Nicholas Roerich Poetry Prize, and *Resistance Fantasies* (Story Line, 2004). Her translation of

Alexis Stamatis's novel, *American Fugue* (Etruscan Press, 2008), received the NEA International Literature Award. Educated at Brown University, she is a Regents' Professor at the University of New Mexico. With her husband and four children, she lives in the foothills of the Sandia Mountains in Albuquerque. Her webpage is www.dianethiel.net.

Thiel writes: "'Listening in Deep Space' is a central poem in my latest collection, *Questions from Outer Space*. The idea of humanity's search for answers and desire for connection is present from the opening lines, as is the recognition of the human impulse to tell stories about ourselves on this journey. The detail of choosing Stravinsky and whale song is a reference to the *Voyager* probes launched in 1977, carrying a record of examples chosen to represent our world. We might intend certain messages as we move through our lives and our art, but these can sometimes be dramatically misconveyed or misinterpreted. As with many pieces in my new book, I gathered the details and images for this poem over years, observing a number of space launches from Cape Canaveral as a native Floridian, visiting sites such as the Very Large Array in New Mexico, and taking my family to space centers and dark skies throughout the world.

"The poem alludes to our troubled human history and the many heinous acts that have been carried out in the name of one particular belief system or another. I was also thinking of interpersonal realms of conflict, which is why houses and home appear in the piece, juxtaposed with continents and oceans. The allusions might serve as reminders, as we move through our contemporary lives, surreal in their swiftly changing dimensions. The poem acknowledges a grim reality based on human history, but with the final line phrased as a question, it also allows room for some pause and some hope."

RODRIGO TOSCANO is a poet and dialogist based in New Orleans. He is the author of ten books of poetry. His latest books are *The Cut Point* (Counterpath, 2023) and *The Charm & The Dread* (Fence Books, 2022). His previous books include *In Range, Explosion Rocks Springfield, Deck of Deeds, Collapsible Poetics Theater* (a National Poetry Series selection) and *To Leveling Swerve, Platform, Partisans,* and *The Disparities*. Toscano won the Edwin Markham 2019 prize for poetry. He works for the Labor Institute in conjunction with the United Steelworkers and the National Institute for Environmental Health Science. See rodrigotoscano.com and @Toscano200.

Toscano writes: " 'Full Haunt' (a sonnet) was written almost a whole year before the two crises in Ukraine (a war) and Taiwan fully unfolded. Possessing a historical-materialist political sensibility (something I have in my intellectual toolkit) could not by itself have achieved this level of prescience. It was only by engaging other poetic thinkers, and looking for clues—in words and phrases, and paying close attention to my own poetic coursing through the unsure waters of the present tense, that 'Full Haunt' came into being. Notable, for me, after that fact of its publication, is the reflexive quality of the poem, its calling attention to its very composition as part of the crises."

TONY TRIGILIO was born in Erie, Pennsylvania, in 1966. His recent books include *Craft: A Memoir* (Marsh Hawk Press, 2023); *Proof Something Happened* (Marsh Hawk, 2021), selected by Susan Howe as winner of the Marsh Hawk Poetry Prize; and *Ghosts of the Upper Floor* (BlazeVOX [books], 2019), the third installment in his multivolume cross-genre project, *The Complete Dark Shadows (of My Childhood)*. A volume of his selected poems was published in Guatemala in 2018 by Editorial Poe (translated by Bony Hernández). He is editor of *Elise Cowen: Poems and Fragments* (Ahsahta Press, 2014) and coeditor of *Visions and Divisions: American Immigration Literature, 1870–1930* (Rutgers University Press, 2008). He cofounded the poetry journal *Court Green* in 2004, and is poetry editor and editor-in-chief of *Allium, A Journal of Poetry & Prose*. Trigilio lives in Chicago, where he is a professor of English and creative writing at Columbia College.

Of "The Steeplejack," Trigilio writes: "As I was rereading Marianne Moore's 'The Steeple-Jack,' long one of my favorite poems of hers, I kept hearing the voices of our current economic crisis speaking to me off-stage. Murmurs of austerity and scarcity interrupted me as I revisited the bucolic seaside town of Moore's poem. I wondered how we'd view Moore's steeplejack today, and if we might be even quicker to spot Moore's skepticism about the poem's New England village charm. Would we see Moore's steeplejack as an artisan, or as merely a 'creative'? How does our contemporary fixation with efficiency and productivity affect our attitudes toward craftspeople like Moore's steeplejack? My conversation with Moore's poem was as much about form as content; I wanted to reimagine her syllabic tensions within the confined space of the sonnet. Moore's poem ends with cautious optimism. Her final word literally is 'hope,' but this feeling is tempered by a sign her steeplejack has placed on the sidewalk in front of the church he's repairing: 'Danger.' Moore's dance between hope and danger is something I echoed in the closing lines of my poem."

DAVID TRINIDAD was born in Los Angeles in 1953. His numerous books include *Digging to Wonderland: Memory Pieces* (Turtle Point Press, 2022), *Notes on a Past Life* (BlazeVOX [books], 2016), *Peyton Place: A Haiku Soap Opera* (Turtle Point, 2013), and *The Late Show* (Turtle Point, 2007). He is also the editor of *A Fast Life: The Collected Poems of Tim Dlugos* (Nightboat Books, 2011), *Punk Rock Is Cool for the End of the World: Poems and Notebooks of Ed Smith* (Turtle Point, 2019), and *Divining Poets: Dickinson*, an Emily Dickinson tarot deck (Turtle Point, 2019). Trinidad lives in Chicago, where he is a professor of English and creative writing at Columbia College.

Of "The Poems Attributed to Him May Be by Different Poets," Trinidad writes: "Each line of the poem is about a different poet that appeared in the *Greek Anthology* of antiquity, arranged alphabetically, beginning with Adaeus and ending with Xenophanes. The sentences were cribbed (and tweaked) from the poets' Wikipedia pages. So I guess you could call this a Wikipedia cento. The poet of the title is Automedon (I just had to do a Google search to identify him)."

ANNE WALDMAN was born in 1945 in Millville, New Jersey, and raised from birth on MacDougal Street in New York City's Greenwich Village. She cofounded the Jack Kerouac School of Disembodied Poetics summer program and MFA at Naropa University. She is the author of more than sixty volumes of poetry and poetics, including *The Iovis Trilogy: Colors in The Mechanism of Concealment* (Coffee House Press, 2011), which won the PEN Center Literary Prize. Penguin published her *Trickster Feminism* (2018) and will publish *Mesopotopia* in 2024. Anne's album *SCIAMACHY* was released in 2020 by Fast Speaking Music and the Lévy Gorvy gallery. She was the keynote speaker for the Bob Dylan and the Beats Conference in Tulsa in Spring 2022.

She wrote the libretto for the opera/movie *Black Lodge*, with music by composer David T. Little, which premiered at Opera Philadelphia in October 2022.

Of "Three Poems from *13 Moons Kora*," Waldman writes: "These poems come from a sequence written over thirteen moons of a year celebrating the birth of child Kora born at the pandemic spring equinox, 2020, across the USA border in Mexico. They are little songs of longing from a grandmother's heart in lockdown. María Sabina 1894–1985: the Mazatec poet and curandera of Huatla, Oaxaca. Kora/Kore/Persephone: daughter of Demeter. 'Junio con patio interno' = 'June with winter yard,' *'Dahlia pinnata'* is the national flower of Mexico, 'topos abuelita' = 'granny moles.'"

SARAH ANNE WALLEN was born in New York City on October 6, 1987. Her full-length book of poetry, *Don't Drink Poison*, was published by United Artists in 2015. She lives in Brooklyn working as a caregiver, publisher (Third Floor Apartment Press), and coeditor (*Poems by Sunday*).

Wallen writes: "'I can see Mars' is a poem I wrote on my balcony in Crown Heights, Brooklyn. It was my birthday, the sky was clear, and I could see Mars. It took a while to decide it was Mars—I thought it was much more likely to be an airplane—but the red dot didn't move at all. Seeing Mars on my birthday made me consider the nature of existence and the reality of planetary movement."

ELIZABETH WILLIS is the author of six books of poetry, most recently *Alive* (New York Review Books, 2015). Her other books include *Address* (Wesleyan University Press, 2011), *Meteoric Flowers* (Wesleyan, 2007), *Turneresque* (Burning Deck, 2003), and *The Human Abstract* (Penguin, 1995). She teaches at the Iowa Writers' Workshop.

Of "And What My Species Did," Willis writes: "This poem began on a walk in the early weeks of the covid pandemic, a time shaped by sudden realignments of relation and risk. There was a new kind of vigilance that cut both ways, driven by competing versions of what—and, more alarmingly, who—is and is not essential in the eyes of whom. I was streaming YouTube videos from China about how to make masks. As the shutdowns began, I could hear sounds that had long been drowned out by the internal and external noise of business as usual. It became impossible not to see the neighborhood as a habitat full of other creatures, human and non-human, mammalian and microscopic, living and dead—and to see every action as touching the realities of the historical and biological whole."

TERENCE WINCH's ninth collection of poems, *That Ship Has Sailed*, was published by the University of Pittsburgh Press in 2023. A Columbia Book Award and American Book Award winner, he has also received an NEA Fellowship and a Gertrude Stein Award for Innovative Writing. Born in the Bronx in 1945 to Irish immigrant parents, Winch is a founding member of the original Celtic Thunder, the Irish band, and composer of the band's best-known song, "When New York Was Irish."

Of "Great Sizzle," Winch writes: "Like most poets, I don't make a practice of analyzing what I write, but when I tried to examine this poem as though it came from someone else, a few thoughts come to mind. The 'sizzle,' I imagine, is simply the hiss of consciousness of the speaker operating at full blast on several levels, from the contemplation of the mundane raking of leaves to the dreamlike encounter with 'embryonic cabbages,' which sound pretty scary. So there seems to be a pairing of the ordinary versus the strange throughout. In fact, I would say that that tension between the mysterious and the commonplace is something that has always captured my attention."

JEFFREY CYPHERS WRIGHT received his MFA after studying with Allen Ginsberg. Best known as a New Romantic poet, he is also a publisher, critic, eco-activist, impresario, singer/songwriter, filmmaker, puppeteer, and artist. His eighteen books of verse include *Blue Lyre* (Dos Madres Press, 2018) and *Party Everywhere* (Xanadu Press, 2020). *Doppelgängster*, a book of sonnets and artwork, is forthcoming from MadHat Press. Wright received a Kathy Acker Award in 2017. He publishes *Live Mag!* www.livemag.org.

Wright writes: "'Sweepstake' is a sonnet that admits the darkness but overshines it. Written during the long lockdown, the poem hints at despair but focuses on bright spots in life: having a mate, duties, and a sense of purpose and belonging. The blessings of love and life become shields of protection.

"There is a natural rhythm to life and this poem captures its cadences, beginning with a frantic pace. Every day IS a holiday if you will it to be, yet every day is also fraught with pressure. Faith is tested and belief renewed as 'unseen guides' keep us whole.

"As the title implies, I feel that it's important to project the persona of a winner and share that positivity. 'Sweepstake' offers balance and perspective, suggesting that winning is more of an attitude than a gamble. These fourteen lines explore the beauty and meaning found in the structures of our 'everyday' lives.

"The reappearance of 'sweep' at the end, as 'Dusk's push broom comes, sweeping us on,' provides a subtle bookend to the title, offering dignity to our own impending conclusion."

JOHN YAU is a poet, art critic, independent curator, and publisher of Black Square Editions. His reviews appear regularly in the online magazine *Hyperallergic*. Among his recent publications are *Joe Brainard: The Art of the Personal* (Rizzoli, 2022), a monograph, and a book of poems, *Genghis Chan on Drums* (Omnidawn, 2021). Forthcoming publications include a selection of essays, *Please Wait by the Coatroom: Reconsidering Race and Identity in American Art* (Black Sparrow, 2023) and a book of poems, *Tell It Slant* (Omnidawn, 2023). An exhibition of his collaborations with artists, organized by Stuart Horodner and The UK Art Museum, is in the works. The recipient of the 2018 Jackson Prize in poetry and the 2021 Rabkin Award in art criticism, Yau lives in New York.

Of "Song for Mie Yim," Yau writes: "In the summer of 2022, I was invited by two guest editors, Susette Min and Amy Sadao, to contribute a piece about the art of Mie Yim, as well as the 'possibilities, future formations, entropic underpinnings of Asian American art' for a special issue of *The Brooklyn Rail*. In an email exchange with Yim, she said that I could send in part of a review of her work that I had written, as the deadline was soon. I did not want to do that. I decided I would write a poem for her, and that it would have something to do with her 'quarantine drawings' of stuffed animal shapes and what she called her 'fragmented identity.' I was not sure who was speaking when I started the poem, except that it was neither me nor the artist. In my mind it was one of Yim's drawings as if I had drawn it."

GEOFFREY YOUNG was born in Los Angeles in 1944, grew up in San Diego, went to college at the University of California, Santa Barbara, and held a Fulbright in France in 1972–73. After eight years in Berkeley, where he and Laura Chester had two sons and founded the small press The Figures, they moved to Great Barrington, Massachusetts, in 1972. After twenty-seven years, Young closed his contemporary art gallery in 2018. *Monk's Mood*, the most recent of his chapbooks of poems and drawings, was printed in December, 2022.

Of "Parallel Bars," Young writes: "In the '70s in Berkeley, we were friends with the poet Stan Rice and his wife, Anne, before she hit big with *Interview with the Vampire*. Why I remember this is bizarre in the extreme, but one night, drinking beer with them, Stan said, 'It gets bad and then it gets worse, and then the bottom falls out,' or something very like that, and for some reason I never forgot the sentiment, the way it sounded. Once I started the poem with that distant memory, it just rolled along, exploiting the periodicity of our emotional lives, for better or worse."

MATTHEW ZAPRUDER was born in Washington, D.C., in 1967. He is the author of five collections of poetry, most recently *Father's Day* (Copper Canyon Press, 2019), as well as two books of prose, *Why Poetry* (Ecco, 2017) and *Story of a Poem: A Memoir* (Unnamed Press, 2023). He teaches in the MFA program in creative writing at Saint Mary's College of California, and is editor at large at Wave Books. He lives in the San Francisco Bay Area with his wife and son. He was the guest editor of *The Best American Poetry 2022*.

Of "The Empty Grave of Zsa Zsa Gabor," Zapruder writes: "When I was a kid, each Saturday night I used to watch *The Love Boat*, an extremely popular show about a luxury cruise ship under the loose yet reassuring authority of Captain Merrill Stubing. Each week, celebrities, most of them film stars from previous decades who I understood to be famous but did not recognize, walked up the gangway to mingle improbably with ordinary folk, occasionally hooking up with them or members of the crew, although we never witnessed any coupling: the cabin door would close, there would be commercials, followed by a scene of the morning after with rumpled hair and awkwardness. I still vividly remember an especially deranged and unforgettable episode in which Stubing's brother (played by the same actor as the Captain, Gavin MacLeod, pronounced Ma-cloud) brings his fiancée aboard, to introduce her to the crew. Zsa Zsa Gabor's character, a former girl-friend of the brother, is also on the ship, and tries to win him back with escalating strategies. Gabor's luxury clothes, good humor, and flair for the dramatic, along with her thick central European accent, made a definite impression on me. In life, Gabor was married nine times, and once famously remarked when asked how many husbands she'd had, 'You mean other than my own?' This poem mentions several titles of movies Gabor starred in. She was bigger than life, and per-haps even greater than death."

MAGAZINES WHERE THE POEMS WERE FIRST PUBLISHED

The Academy of American Poets Poem-a-Day, guest ed. John Murillo. www.poets.org

AGNI, poetry eds. Jennifer Kwon Dobbs, Jessica Q. Stark, Esteban Rodriguez, Dorsey Craft, and Jenny George. www.agnionline.bu.edu

Allium, A Journal of Poetry & Prose, editor-in-chief and poetry ed. Tony Trigilio. www.allium.colum.edu

The American Poetry Review, editor-in-chief Elizabeth Scanlon. www.aprweb.org

Bennington Review, ed. Michael Dumanis. www.benningtonreview.org

The Best American Poetry Blog, ed. David Lehman. www.blog.bestamericanpoetry.com

Big Other, ed. John Madera. www.bigother.com

Birmingham Poetry Review, ed. Adam Vines. www.uab.edu/cas/englishpublications/bpr

Biscuit Hill, eds. Elijah Rushing Hayes, Delia Pless, and Chris Hunt Griggs. www.thebiscuithill.com

BOMB, managing ed. Benjamin Samuel, editor-in-chief Betsy Sussler. www.bombmagazine.org

The Brooklyn Rail, poetry ed. Anselm Berrigan. www.brooklynrail.org

The Café Review, poetry ed. Craig Sipe. www.thecafereview.com

The Common, poetry ed. John Hennessy. www.thecommononline.org

Conjunctions, ed. Bradford Morrow. www.conjunctions.com

Court Green, eds. Aaron Smith and Tony Trigilio. www.courtgreen.net

Gulf Coast, poetry eds. Sarah Cunningham, Anthony Sutton, KT Herr, and Jari Bradley. www.gulfcoastmag.org

Hanging Loose, eds. Dick Lourie, Mark Pawlak, Caroline Hagood, Jiwon Choi, and Joanna Fuhrman. www.hangingloosepress.com

Harper's, poetry ed. Ben Lerner. www.harpers.org

Harvard Review, poetry ed. Major Jackson. www.harvardreview.org

Iterant, editor-in-chief Walter J. Stone. www.iterant.org

Live Mag!, publisher and ed. Jeffrey Cyphers Wright. www.livemag.org

London Review of Books, eds. Jean McNicol and Alice Spawls. www.lrb.co.uk

Marsh Hawk Review, publisher Sandy McIntosh, guest ed. Daniel Morris. www.marshhawkpress.org

Mississippi Review, editor-in-chief Adam Clay. www.sites.usm.edu/mississippi-review

New American Writing, ed. Paul Hoover. www.newamericanwriting.com

The New York Review of Books, executive ed. Jana Prikryl. www.nybooks.com

The New York Times Magazine, poetry ed. Victoria Chang. www.nytimes.com/section/magazine

The New Yorker, poetry ed. Kevin Young. www.newyorker.com

The Paris Review, poetry ed. Srikanth Reddy. www.theparisreview.org

Plume, editor-in-chief Daniel Lawless. www.plumepoetry.com

Poetry, ed. Adrian Metejka. www.poetryfoundation.org/poetrymagazine

Poetry Daily, www.poets.com

Prelude, eds. Stu Watson and Armando Jaramillo Garcia. www.preludemag.com

A Public Space, poetry ed. Brett Fletcher Lauer. www.publicspace.org

Raritan Quarterly, editor-in-chief Jackson Lears. www.raritanquarterly.rutgers.edu

South Florida Poetry Journal, poetry eds. Judy Ireland and Meryl Stratford. www.southfloridapoetryjournal.com

Tablet, literary ed. David Samuels. www.tabletmag.com

Three Fold, poetry ed. Chris Tysh. www.threefoldpress.org

Tupelo Quarterly, poetry eds. José Felipe Alvergue, Ruth Awad, Rebecca Hazelton, Catherine Imbriglio, and Simone Muench. www.tupeloquarterly.com

Virginia Quarterly Review, poetry ed. Gregory Pardlo. www.vqronline.org

Vox Populi, eds. Michael Simms and Dr. Nisha Gupta. www.voxpopulisphere.com

Wet Cement Press Magazine, eds. Thoreau Lovell, Barbara Roether, and Michelle Murphy. www.wetcementpress.com/wcpmag

ACKNOWLEDGMENTS

The series editor wishes to thank Mark Bibbins for his many invaluable contributions. Warm thanks go also to Kate Farrell, Caroline Hagood, Major Jackson, Stacey Lehman, Jerome Sala, Mary Jo Salter, Lindsay Shapiro, and Terence Winch; to Glen Hartley and Lynn Chu of Writers' Representatives; and to Kathy Belden, David Stanford Burr, Daniel Cuddy, Kathryn Kenney-Peterson, Rebekah Jett, and Mia O'Neill at Scribner. The poetry editors of the magazines that were our sources deserve applause; they are the secret heroes of contemporary poetry.

Grateful acknowledgment is made of the magazines in which these poems first appeared and the magazine editors who selected them. A sincere attempt has been made to locate all copyright holders. Unless otherwise noted, copyright to the poems is held by the individual poets.

Boris Dralyuk, "Days at the Races" from *Raritan Quarterly*. Reprinted by permission of the poet.

Joanna Fuhrman, "330 College Avenue" from *South Florida Poetry Journal*. Reprinted by permission of the poet.

Amy Gerstler, "Night Herons" from *The New Yorker*. Reprinted by permission of the poet.

Peter Gizzi, "Revisionary" from *The New York Review of Books*. Reprinted by permission of the poet.

Herbert Gold, "Other News on Page 24" from *Tablet*. Reprinted by permission of the poet.

Terrance Hayes, "Strange as the Rules of Grammar" from *The Paris Review*. Reprinted by permission of the poet.

Robert Hershon, "All Right" from *Hanging Loose*. Reprinted by permission of Hanging Loose Press.

Paul Hoover, "Admonitions, Afternoons" from *Allium, A Journal of Poetry & Prose*. Reprinted by permission of the poet.

Shelley Jackson, "Best Original Enigma in Verse" from *Conjunctions*. Reprinted by permission of the poet.

Patricia Spears Jones, "The Devil's Wife Explains Broken 45s" from *Vox Populi*. Reprinted by permission of the poet.

Ilya Kaminsky, "I Ask That I Do Not Die" from *Poetry*. Reprinted by permission of the poet.

Vincent Katz, "A Marvelous Sky" from *Hanging Loose*. Reprinted by permission of the poet.

John Keene, "Straight, No Chaser" from *Punks: New & Selected Poems*. © 2021 by John Keene. Reprinted by permission of The Song Cave. Also appeared in *BOMB*.

Miho Kinnas, "Three Shrimp Boats on the Horizon" from *Wet Cement Press Magazine*. Reprinted by permission of the poet.